VESLEY MOON, INC. **WHITE WEBB, LLC.** ALLY CO
TONINO BUZZETTA DESIGN **ASHLEY** BA
**OSTROM & ASSOCIATES** BITTT GROUP **B** RN
RNEN DESIGN **BRADFIELD & TOBIN** BRETT DESIG
S CAPITAL C INTERIORS **CHAD JAMES GROUP** CH
**OSS, LLC.** CULLMAN & KRAVIS, INC. **DARRIN VA**
Y GUILLAUME GENTET, INC. **DONNA LIVINGSTON**
INTERIORS **EILEEN KATHRYN BOYD INTERIORS** EL
**RIC COHLER DESIGN** GARY MCBOURNIE, INC. **HA**
**UNIFORD DESIGN STUDIO** HUNTLEY & CO. INTERIO
**ONS** INGRAO, INC. **INSON DUBOIS WOOD, LLC.** JA
OHLER MASON DESIGN **JOLIE KOREK & CO.** JOY
SHAULIS, INC. **LILLIAN AUGUST** MABLEY HANDL
**X CREATIVE** MARSHALL WATSON INTERIORS **M**
E ROY DESIGN **MICHAEL TAVANO DESIGN** PAMELA
**ESIGN** PATRICK JAMES HAMILTON DESIGNS **PA**
K LÖNN DESIGN **PAULA + MARTHA, LLC.** PAVARI
**ANNE EASON** RACHEL LAXER INTERIORS **RC STU**
N **RIO HAMILTON** ROBERT PASSAL INTERIOR & A
URAL DESIGN **RYAN KORBAN** SASHA BIKOFF IN
**A MAGEL** THOM FILICIA, INC. **TIMOTHY BROWN S**
CREATIVE **TOBI FAIRLEY INTERIOR DESIGN** 2 MIC
**, INC.** VICENTE WOLF ASSOCIATES, INC. **WEITZ**
WESLEY MOON, INC. **WHITE WEBB, LLC.** ALLY CO
TONINO BUZZETTA DESIGN **ASHLEY DARRYL** BA

HOLIDAY
HOUSE

# HOLIDAY HOUSE

## TEN YEARS OF DECORATING FOR A CURE

IRIS DANKNER

TEXT BY PATRICK J. HAMILTON

FOREWORD BY CHRISTOPHER HYLAND

POINTED LEAF PRESS, LLC.

CHANEL

# CONTENTS

# FOREWORD

## CHRISTOPHER HYLAND

Rooms are empty vessels.

Rooms await embellishment.

Iris Dankner gives them meaning.

Holiday House is the way.

Decorators—for a decade and counting!—have risen to the occasion, creating Holiday House: several hundred rooms that scintillate, moving our aesthetic sense to new experiences, new horizons.

The frontiers of design we visit at Holiday House satiate our love affair with objects, with their placement in the rooms they inhabit. Most important, in the doing, these exquisite rooms raise funds to combat the scourge of cancer, in particular, for The Breast Cancer Research Foundation®, founded by Evelyn Lauder.

As I write this Foreword, I am composing the lyrics for a large musical composition celebrating the extraordinary American narrative of hope, courage, and tenacity—the same spirit of can-do, of perseverance, of vision—evinced by Iris Dankner, who survived breast cancer, and by the designers who contribute their skills toward eradicating this terrible disease. I have been honored these many years to be both, with Iris, the Chairperson of Holiday House, and now, its Chairman.

Geographical boundaries might be crossed but the boundaries within us, emotional and spiritual, are still to be explored, are still to be extended. Holiday House traverses boundaries. It meshes the realms of fantasy and desire with those of the practical and informative. It educates us about the extraordinary human ability to conceive abstractly and transform that daydream to the tangible phenomenon of place.

Each year at Holiday House, I am reminded of my New England roots, that sense of community, of purpose, of Town Meetings assembled in pursuit of the good. Holiday House is like a barn-raising, the coming together of neighbors to build.

Annually in New York City and in the Hamptons, an array of the most accomplished decorators gathers their most refined and exciting design visions, resulting in a roundup of the best in interior design: Holiday House opens to thousands of visitors who now comprise a loyal, enthusiastic, and committed following to whom Iris, her steadfast staff, and the decorators are grateful.

Decorative vision is naked without the materials to realize it, affording the hundreds of home furnishing companies who contribute their products to Holiday House both a dramatic showcase and an opportunity to participate in a fundamental human tenet: Charity.

In the long view of my life, the voices of Holiday House—manifest both in literal conversation, the nod of a head, a wink, a smile, a unique gesture, as well as in the language of design present in each room—will resound because Holiday House exhorts us to soar, to bring to fruition artistic aspiration. What more noble cause than to realize beauty?

Life's travails aside, in the art of Holiday House rooms we discover not only beauty but the fulfillment of aspiration, a constant truth. Most importantly, in the rooms of Holiday House, we find the affirmation of place, of home; that sanctuary from the tumult of the world.

Join us in this tome, this memento of life through rooms.

The many splendid rooms of Holiday House.

# INTRODUCTION

## IRIS DANKNER

As a little girl, I was the colorful black sheep of the family. My sister is a therapist and my brother is a doctor, and I was always the artist. Taking art classes, making things, always made me so happy. Now my love of interior design makes absolute sense. Although back then, it just meant that when my brother and sister were studying, I was in my room moving my furniture and redecorating.

While my brother and sister were starting their medical educations, my dad took me around to look at art schools. I was accepted into both Cornell and Carnegie Mellon School of Art. Everyone was so excited that I got into Cornell. "Now you can meet an Ivy League husband!" they'd joke. But I wanted to be an artist. So off to Carnegie Mellon I went.

After graduation, my first job back in the city was at Lord & Taylor, where I advanced to Art Director and stayed for 13 years. When my second daughter was born, I decided to take some time off. At a Mommy & Me class, I met my friend Emily Hochberg. After a play date in my apartment, she looked around and said, "When I move into a house, I want you to decorate it." Two years later, Emily bought her first big, beautiful home on Long Island and, true to her word, she called me in to design it. That's when my next career started. I went back to school, this time the New York School of Interior Design, and I was on my way to a career as an interior designer. I spent 12 years designing and redesigning Emily's home, growing my client list along the way. Life was good! But life is funny.

February 18th, 1997, started out as a typical day. I woke up and made myself a cup of coffee before I woke my daughters, Danielle and Niki. I sipped my coffee and read my datebook to see what my schedule was. Business as usual: 10:00 am, client appointment. Noon, lunch date. 1:00 pm, my first routine mammogram. Pick up the girls at 3:15, then play dates and afterschool activities. Totally typical. But little did I know that at that one o'clock mammogram, my life would change forever. I heard the dreaded words: "You have breast cancer."

The year after my diagnosis was physically overwhelming and emotionally intense, but with amazing doctors, and the strength and love of my husband, daughters, family, and friends, I came out on the other side. Early detection saved my life.

Before my cancer diagnosis, I was living the perfect, if naïve, life: handsome, successful husband, two beautiful, healthy daughters, and my own business as an interior designer. After my treatment and surgeries, people would say to me, "Now you can get back to normal!" *Normal*. What was "normal" now? I needed to redefine what it meant for me. And cancer changed how "normal" would now be defined.

As much as I loved it, and my clients, I couldn't go back to just decorating. While my love of design remained, my perspective had certainly changed. I couldn't bear listening to complaints about things like the trim on a pillow or how a paint color was a shade off. Even my life as a mother had changed. I couldn't just sit and talk about clothes, homework and afterschool activities. Cancer made me realize that I needed something bigger. While my amazing doctors made me cancer-free and also put me back together (with a new, perky set of "girls"!), now I needed to find a way to heal emotionally.

Six months after my surgery, early on a Sunday morning, Jay, Danielle, Niki and my dear friend Mindy—all of us dressed in pink—walked our first Susan G. Komen Race for the Cure. I walked and I was moved. I walked and I cried. I walked and I laughed. I read all the placards with names of women who were not as lucky as I was to survive, and alongside all of the women who were.

The next year, I invited friends and family to join me at the Race for the Cure and "Iris' Bosom Buddies" was born. Over the next few years, we grew to over 120 strong, and were the highest fundraising team of the walk. It made me feel so good, and like I was part of a larger community.

I never set out to make my life about fundraising. It just happened because it helped me heal. And while I was healing, I was helping others.

So *this* would be my new normal: helping others, and paying it forward. Before I knew it, I was on the board of Susan G. Komen and chairing the Race for the Cure in NYC. Gathering over 20,000 people in Central Park to walk for a common cause was truly unbelievable. Standing on the stage, watching the walkers, and feeling all that positive energy, the healing continued, surrounded by a sea of pink.

But cancer doesn't affect just the patient: It affects the entire family. My two daughters shared with me at age 15 and 18 how scared, alone, and helpless they felt. They wanted to help other kids who were feeling the same way. That's when they created *Tickled Pink*, a fundraiser for survivors and their children. They raised over a million dollars and helped other kids deal with watching their moms go through treatment for breast cancer. Through *Tickled Pink*, my daughters taught me how to put the "fun" back in "fundraising." I couldn't have been prouder.

After three years of chairing the Race for the Cure in Manhattan, I was asked to join a group of delegates going to the Race for the Cure in Egypt. We walked from the pyramids to the Sphinx, alongside women in hijabs, some wearing survivor T-shirts pinned to their burqas. At that moment, I realized cancer knows no boundaries, spares no faith, and doesn't discriminate.

I asked Nancy Brinker, the founder of Susan G. Komen, "Why did you do the Race for the Cure in Egypt before doing one in Israel?" She answered, "You want to work on one in Israel? Go right ahead!" So for the next 12 months, I worked on the Race for the Cure in Jerusalem. Working with the Knesset, selecting a production company, and even walking the route with the mayor to make sure we had the security we needed. This time, I watched Arabs and Israelis walking side by side toward a common cause, and with only one enemy: Cancer. At the end of the walk, as the sun was setting, we turned the Wailing Wall pink. It was one of the most amazing experiences of my life.

And through it all, I was still designing. I realized I had two full-time jobs: I was a full-time interior designer *and* a full-time fundraiser. And I loved both of my lives.

Although the interior design community was generally a charitable one, there were no events or fundraisers in the industry to benefit any women's issues. That was my proverbial "Aha!" moment. That's when I had the dream of creating Holiday House, a designer showhouse that would benefit breast cancer research. This would be how I would combine my two passions: my love of interior design, and my passion to eradicate breast cancer.

Designer showhouses are a great and grand tradition in the interior design world in the U.S. An empty home is transformed, room by room, by established and up-and-coming interior designers who bring along an army of vendors and volunteers donating their time, talent, and wares to turn empty spaces into show-stopping, magazine-worthy designs.

These rooms, hallways, and stair landings (and even the closets!) become the backdrops for fundraising galas and visitors, other design enthusiasts, fellow survivors, and their families.

Our years at the Academy Mansion really were a showcase of the pure and utter transformative power of design, since for those ten years, Holiday House designers showed what paint, paper, and creativity could do to change a space, even if the rooms themselves stayed the same year after year. As we grew and branched out to the Hamptons and then SoHo, the designers' power to transform shaped new construction and brought new audiences to the Holiday House story.

And, wow, do our designers make it look easy! But what in life is ever as easy as it seems on the surface? Yet through the delivery mix-ups, the occasional blown fuses, the jockeying for the freight elevator (or stairway), the outrageously short set-up schedules, and amid all the controlled chaos, it's not just the house that's transformed. What starts as an alphabetical listing of designers, workrooms, stylists, landscape artists, and design firms becomes something different: It becomes a family. While it turns empty rooms into jewel boxes, it turns friendly competitors into life-long friends. All in the name of fundraising. All in the name of healing.

The name "Holiday House" came from my own feeling that after you've had cancer, every day is a gift, every day is a holiday. Over the years, the name has also triggered room designs inspired by holidays, special occasions and dates on the calendar, some of which you'll discover in the pages that follow. It's given each year a festive, celebratory feel. You walk through Holiday House, and you see the creativity. And you feel the love. I hope you'll also feel the love on these very pages.

In the summer of 2014, we were installing our second annual showhouse in the Hamptons when a designer backed out two weeks before the opening of the show. As I like to say, sometimes management needs to step up to the plate. So that I did, and I created a beautiful beach bungalow room inspired by beachy artwork. In the winter of 2014 in our annual NYC showhouse, I created a magical room to celebrate my daughter's engagement. What better way to celebrate her tying the knot than by creating the ultimate bridal dressing room? This room was very meaningful to me because when I was sick, I remember thinking to myself, "I just want to live to see my daughters get married."

The beauty of Holiday House is not just the money we raise for breast cancer research. It's also the lives it touches. From editors and publishers, to the painters and contractors, making Holiday House about breast cancer has revealed how so many lives are touched by that dreaded C word, as mine was that February day. So many had a story they wanted to share. I've been moved many times by these personal stories, from visitors and vendors, and even burly delivery guys and tough construction workers who tell me, with a tear in their eye, how moms, sisters, and wives were affected by cancer... and how good it felt to give back and dedicate a moment to these courageous women.

My Holiday House dream has really grown more than I could ever imagine. We're crossing the Atlantic and going to London in the fall of 2017, opening the very first Holiday House abroad. We're helping to introduce the whole showhouse concept to a British audience, with some of the country's top designers. Working with The Breast Cancer Research Foundation® has been one of the most rewarding parts of my journey, knowing that 99 cents of every dollar we raise goes to funding new research projects.

Last year, at a high school reunion, a woman I hadn't seen in about 20 years asked me, "Is your life really as perfect as it looks on Facebook?" My first thought was, "Yeah, right!" We're all guilty of it, I suppose...cherry-picking the best and the most beautiful moments, like family vacations, weddings, girls' nights out, memorable meals, and picture-perfect sunsets. But we sometimes gloss over the not-so-good stuff. I didn't post when my dad was diagnosed with colon cancer. I didn't upload any shots after they removed part of my mom's lung to cure her lung cancer. And there were no selfies when I sat with my sister during 36 hours of chemo with a penguin cap after her diagnosis of cancer. Then I stopped, took a breath and responded, "You know what—it *is* as perfect as it looks." We've all had our ups and downs, and I often say it's not the cards you're dealt, but how you play the hand. Life is not always easy, but I'm blessed to always be surrounded by my incredible family and friends, and the incredible people I have met along my journey. Truthfully, what could be better? That seems pretty picture-perfect to me.

Ultimately, my story and the story of Holiday House are both about the transformative power of design. We start with an empty house, and we bring it to life, doing what we do as designers: deciding floor plans, picking colors, hanging drapes and wallpaper, placing the perfect piece of art, creating comfort, and creating beauty. Each time we start a new house, we start with a list of designers, and we turn them into family, with bonds that might be made from paint, paper, and fabric, but turn out to be as strong as blood. We may start feeling helpless in the face of cancer, but we end up making something beautiful. And we end up making a real difference. The phrase "labor of love" gets thrown around, but that's really what Holiday House is.

This book is just the latest chapter in the story, a brief (and beautiful) moment to reflect on the generosity, the creativity, the passion, the inspiration, and the healing Holiday House brings, to me and to so many. Let the journey, the creativity, the healing, and the holidays all continue. These aren't just gorgeous rooms. These are rooms that embrace, celebrate, and champion. These are rooms that take us one step closer to a cure.

FARROW&BALL

# THE ACADEMY MANSION, NEW YORK

It is a wide and handsome facade, stone-faced in construction and demeanor, not overly showy by the standards of its Gilded Age elder cousins or even its contemporary neighbors. The first impression is a bit like being handed a simple envelope with a modest wax seal that hints at something special inside.

Only when opened are its contents revealed, an invitation to a festive soirée unfolding with flourish, pattern, and ornament. Arched double doors framed by carved medallions are the only clues to the secrets inside the Academy Mansion, just steps away from Manhattan's Central Park.

One of those secrets, an interior courtyard, makes this house unique among the many fine homes populating Manhattan's Upper East Side. Built by the British-born American architect Frederick Sterner in 1920 for William Ziegler, Jr., a prominent businessman and his wife Gladys, the structure spans three lots, enabling a first-floor plan akin to that of a Roman villa. The central square is surrounded by a large parlor and dining room, linked by the dramatic curve of the main staircase landing at one end and an intimate study at the other.

The scale of its upstairs spaces is tamer, but by no means humble. The fourth floor, hidden from street view, holds another surprise: a ballroom with the feel of a solarium, replete with a skylight and more arched windows.

Even bare, these rooms are grand and detailed, good bones awaiting their party clothes. There are stone octagons paving the foyer, a barrel vault with trailing vines of plaster, Palladian windows, deeply carved paneling, stained-glass windows, and head-high fireplaces, with parts and pieces imported from noble homes in Tuscany and England. And everywhere, a quarry's worth of limestone.

Since the Academy Mansion hosted its first Holiday House in 2007, these details have provided both inspiration and challenge to the designers who were eager to put their stamp on rooms sometimes full of immutable details.

## THE ENTRANCE FOYER

## THE PARLOR

MARCEL PROUST
SWANN'S WAY

AFRICA
BALLETS RUSSES

ARABIAN HORSES

## THE LIBRARY



2015: The *Boxing Day* room featured intimate, multi-functional zones, mixing contemporary upholstery with antiques, and using dusky-hued pastels to soften the masculine space.



2014: Pale and mostly monochromatic elements serve as counterpoints to the *Celebration of the Holidays*—dark paneling, with stronger colors reserved for the contemporary oil painting.



2013: Mixed metaphors of the global kind for *A Swede in Scottish Holiday Spirit*, incorporated the designer's Swedish heritage and Scottish textiles to create a room decorated for the Christmas holidays.

The Scottish World
DISCO YEARS RON GALELLA

NEW YORK APARTMENTS
MAURICE FATIO

DESIGNERS AT HOME
Private Gardens of Connecticut
HAIR
MANNAHATTA
TRADITIONAL HOME

1000 Nudes
740 PARK

HELMUT NEWTON
Leonardo da Vinci
ARABIAN HORSES

## THE DINING ROOM

BE MY GUEST
VATICAN
SIMPLY ITALIAN
CIPRIANI
RENZO MONGIARDINO
NARDI
PICASSO

## THE MASTER BEDROOM

## THE SITTING ROOM

THE DETAILED INTERIOR
THE DETAILED INTERIOR

OLIVER MESSEL

GIO PONTI
LA MAMOUNIA
ASSOULINE
OSCAR NIGHT

BLACK • WHITE
LOUIS VUITTON MARC JACOBS
CHANEL
TOM FORD
GUCCI BY GUCCI
YVES SAINT LAURENT STYLE

FURNITURE

KAGAN

## THE FRONT BEDROOM

Classic Rooms
SENSATIONAL BOUQUETS
The Well-Lived Life
THE HAMPTONS

AVEDON FASHION

## THE HOME OFFICE

THE LIGHT OF NEW YORK
LIVING IN STYLE LONDON
LIVING IN STYLE PARIS
WILLIAM KLEIN PARIS + KLEIN
BERENICE ABBOTT
TOM FORD

CHAGALL
HISTORY OF MODERN ART
DOMESTIC AR
HOTELS

## THE GUEST BEDROOM

ALEXANDER McQUEEN: SAVAGE BEAUTY
LOUIS VUITTON

THE LIGHT OF NEW YORK
THE LIGHT OF TOKYO
THE LIGHT OF VENICE
THE LIGHT OF ISTANBUL
THE LIGHT OF PARIS
HOTEL STORIES

LOOK
SHARP.
AMERICAN FASHION
THE LITTLE BLACK JACKET
MEYER

DOISNEAU
TASCHEN

## THE TOP-FLOOR BALLROOM

DREAM
SOWHAT!
GIANTS

# THE HAMPTONS, NEW YORK

In the summer of 2013, Holiday House did for the first time what elite Manhattanites have done for generations—head for the Hamptons on Long Island.

With roots reaching back into the 1600s, Hamptons history is populated by river otters and harbor porpoises, Algonquin Indians and Dutch settlers, whalers, sailors and potato farmers, then Fords and DuPonts, writers, producers, and polo players. With its transition from humble to chic, the Hamptons have become one of the nation's toniest year-round addresses.

But it's the months between Memorial and Labor days that the Hamptons hit their stride: Homes reopened for the season, population swelling with bold-faced names and suntanned faces.

This ribbon of towns and hamlets at the East End of Long Island has become a playground for architects, too, who embrace, reinterpret or eschew vernacular styles, reworking the classic shingled saltbox to grand proportion or dotting the sand dunes with minimal, shining glass boxes.

The first Holiday House Hamptons found a home in Bridgehampton. The 7,900-square-foot residence was developed by the Villadom Corporation at Bridgehampton, and designers took inspiration from local history, the beachy locale, and iconic Hamptons summer style.

The second Holiday House location, in 2014, took up residence in Sag Harbor, and was the Hamptons' first resort-style luxury condominium project. Watchcase, created by Curtis Bashaw and Craig Wood's Cape Advisors, was an inventive repurposing of a local 130-year-old landmark. Designers worked within this unique, lofty framework in three separate homes, viewing their seaside inspiration through a decidedly urban lens.

Holiday House returned to the Hamptons again in 2016, to the hamlet of Watermill. The modern estate on Mecox Bay was designed by Philip Rossillo at PRDG architecture + design, and built by John DeVito at 456 Development Group. It boasted a rooftop tennis court with ocean views, merging the very best of Hamptons lifestyles. All three Hamptons houses were presented in partnership with *Hamptons Cottages & Gardens*.

The Hamptons designers took cues from the classic style of this uniquely American summer escape, and inspiration from each distinctive architectural framework. Like their Holiday House city counterparts, they brought personal vision and fresh perspectives to dates and days on the calendar that are worth celebrating.

## WATERMILL 2016

### MADDUX CREATIVE 140

*Cornwall Coastline*, a contemporary riff on traditional board-and-batten, painted in a coastal spectrum of Farrow & Ball colors, proved a foil to the main staircase's traditional woodwork in the crisp and arty entry foyer.

### HB HOME 142

The white stucco of Mediterranean architecture provided dazzling inspiration for *Party in Pantelleria,* a soothing, lounge-like space, channeling the exclusive Sicilian island escape.

### MABLEY HANDLER INTERIOR DESIGN 144

School's out in this *Graduation Day* seaside game room, where classic blue-and-white took an artful twist, with watercolor murals by Phillip Jeffries.

### CHAD JAMES GROUP 148

Moody and clubby, *May Day,* a ground-floor sitting room, provided the perfect place for a nightcap or relaxing on a rainy day.

### BALTIMORE DESIGN GROUP 150

All things organic provided the inspiration for *Harvest East End*, a space with botanicals, a tree-trunk sculpture, a fossil side table, and moss green upholstery, all a nod to the area's agrarian roots.

### 2 MICHAELS DESIGN 152

With pared-down global reference and contemporary photography, Jayne and Joan Michaels' *International Woman's Day* was a lyric space that mixed shape, line, and texture.

### TIMOTHY BROWN STUDIO 154

Heroically scaled modern artwork provided a contemplative anchor for *Father's Day,* a room with a flexible, floating seating arrangement.

### JOLIE KOREK & CO. 156

*Summer Solstice,* the longest day of the year, didn't seem quite long enough when you visited this bedroom, where wooden floors are kept bare to highlight the more opulent bedlinens.

### WESLEY MOON, INC. 158

It's a *Palm Sunday* of a different kind, as the designer was inspired by a graphic date-palm print, used like a modern toile on both the bed's soaring canopy and the room's entry walls.

### MELANIE ROY DESIGN 160

*Earth Day* gets a glamorous reimagining in both a textural, spa-like bedroom, where feathers, inlaid bedside tables, and a luxurious shag rug soften the more architectural lines, as well as on an expansive sheltered deck, where a modern take on a porch swing is just one of the seating options in the multi-use, summer-perfect space.

### BARBARA OSTROM & ASSOCIATES 164

You didn't have to go far to enjoy an entire season's worth of activity in this artfully packed *Staycation Day* space, a fanciful mix of summer fun in the mansion's multi-purpose garage/playroom.

SHAFFER

ED RUSCHA
BILL OWENS
MAX ERNST
ELLSWORTH KELLY
PRESTEL
STERLING RUBY
GAGOSIAN HONGKONG

PORSCHE

## BRIDGEHAMPTON 2013

BECKER
VANITY FAIR

MAKING MARKS
GOLF RESORTS
ARCADIAN ARCHITECTURE
"Dialog"
JUAN USLÉ
JANSEN

YVES

HAMPTONS HAVENS

HAMPTONS GARDENS
HOUSES IN MY HEART
Decorating Master Class
LIVING TRADITIONS

Static Reduce
Drum Light
Cycle Signal
Control Lock
SensorDrying

Marie Antoinette

## SAG HARBOR 2014

**HUNIFORD DESIGN STUDIO** 192

*Labor Day* set a swinging tone to this living room that was one part lounge, one part loft, but all earthy and eclectic, with tailored upholstery and vintage treasures.

**BJØRNEN DESIGN** 194

Take a lap in *Seahorse Country,* a watery-blue family room, where barn meets beach with a monochromatic color scheme to keep it nice and calm, and textures to make things interesting.

**ID CREATIONS** 196

A breezy Hamptons style is effortlessly and stylishly captured in *Bungalow* by showhouse founder Iris Dankner, where Pop Art flowers gave big-city panache to a cottage-like space.

Mark Rothko
CY TWOMBLY

VERA WANG ON WEDDINGS
An EVENT to REMEMBER
FORTUNY

# SULLIVAN MANSIONS, NEW YORK

Two townhomes, side by side in SoHo. Each with its own front stoop, tucked back from the sidewalk. On the landings, from the front door, a view straight through to a back yard decked with greenery. Off to one side, a stairway leading to three more floors above.

For the luckiest in Manhattan, it's a familiar setting. But these handsome twins, more fraternal than identical, are not typical brownstones. These are thoroughly modern mansions.

The units are two in a row of five comprising the Sullivan Mansions, sitting on an unusual triangular parcel of land, an island within the bigger island of Manhattan, and the fleeting home to Holiday House 2016. The project was developed by Property Markets Group and Madison Equities, New York-based real estate development firms that have reimagined properties for nearly a quarter of a century.

Designed by New York architects Cary Tamarkin and Montroy Andersen DeMarco, the exteriors and interior spaces are judicious in their built-in detail, spare but elegant, with more right angles than curves, except for the sweep of the staircases. In bathrooms and kitchens, materials, not moldings, take center stage.

The townhouses bring the grace of New York past in a brand new way to the bustling, stylish neighborhood of SoHo (short for "South of Houston," the nearby street of neighborhood demarcation), known more for its artists' studios, printing plants, and cast-iron facades than for actual old school townhome living. The lofty, industrial past of the neighborhood eases in, though, through windows of flat-stock black metal, framing the Manhattan sky views like Mondrians.

Like the Hamptons locations, but unlike the Academy Mansion, these buildings were brand new when the Holiday House designers moved in, bringing layers and life to the rooms inside with their usual toolkits: textiles, antiques, color, texture, artwork, and a very determined vision.

# SOHO 2016

PLENTY
ENTERTAINING

BEATON
THE ART OF THE SCRAPBOOK
BEATON
ASSOULINE

AGNES MARTIN

VERUSCHKA

RYAN KORBAN
RYAN KORBAN
RYAN KORBAN
LUXURY REDEFINED
RYAN KORBAN

# THE DESIGNERS

PAGES 34-35, 54-55, 130-131
**ALLY COULTER**
**ALLY COULTER DESIGNS**
51 BELLEVUE AVENUE
NEWPORT, RI 02840
(646) 785-6405
WWW.ALLYCOULTER.COM

PAGES 32-33
**AMY LAU**
**AMY LAU DESIGN**
601 WEST 26TH STREET, SUITE M272
NEW YORK, NY 10001
(212) 645-6168
WWW.AMYLAUDESIGN.COM

PAGES 92-93
**ANTONINO BUZZETTA**
**ANTONINO BUZZETTA DESIGN**
39 WEST 14TH STREET, SUITE 504
NEW YORK, NY 10011
(917) 971-0571
WWW.ANTONINOBUZZETTA.COM

PAGES 104-105
**ASHLEY DARRYL**
NEW YORK CITY
(214) 232-1676
WWW.INTERIORS.ASHLEYDARRYL.COM

PAGES 150-151
**KEITH BALTIMORE**
**BALTIMORE DESIGN GROUP**
35 MAIN STREET
PORT WASHINGTON, NY 11050
(516) 944-2400
WWW.BALTIMOREDESIGNCENTER.COM

PAGES 90-91, 164-165, 206-207
**BARBARA OSTROM & MEREDITH OSTROM**
**BARBARA OSTROM & ASSOCIATES**
1 INTERNATIONAL BLVD, 209
MAHWAH, NJ 07495
(201) 529-0444
WWW.BARBARAOSTROM.NET

PAGE 4
**SHERRI SKOV, BONNIE STEVES, LANA LAWRENCE,**
(ABOVE), **ANGELA SMITH, & NINA HELMS**
**BITTT GROUP (BONNIE J. STEVES)**
217 EAST 70TH STREET
NEW YORK, NY 10021
(646) 678-4450
WWW.BJS-ASSOC.COM

PAGES 52-53
**BJÖRN BJÖRNSSON**
**BJÖRN BJÖRNSSON INTERIOR DESIGN, LLC.**
345 EAST 52ND STREET, 7D
NEW YORK, NY 10022
(212) 207-4980
WWW.BJORNBJORNSSON.COM

PAGES 194-195
**JOHN BJØRNEN**
**BJØRNEN DESIGN**
144 MAIN STREET
SAG HARBOR, NY 11963
(631) 725-0946
WWW.BJORNENDESIGN.COM

PAGES 26-27, 210-211
**GEOFFREY BRADFIELD AND RORIC TOBIN**
**BRADFIELD & TOBIN**
116 EAST 61ST STREET
NEW YORK, NY 10065
(212) 758-1773
WWW.GEOFFREYBRADFIELD.COM

PAGES 116-117
**BRETT BELDOCK**
**BRETT DESIGN, INC.**
201 EAST 87TH STREET
NEW YORK, NY 10128
(212) 987-8270
WWW.BRETTDESIGNINC.COM

PAGES 60-61, 208-209
**CAMPION PLATT**
**CAMPION PLATT INTERIORS**
152 MADISON AVENUE
NEW YORK, NY 10016
(212) 779-3835
WWW.CAMPIONPLATT.COM

PAGES 214-215
**JUAN CARRETERO**
**CAPITAL C INTERIORS**
23 EAST 7TH STREET, GROUND FLOOR
NEW YORK, NY 10003
(212) 228-0468
WWW.CAPITALCINTERIORS.COM

PAGES 148-149
**CHAD JAMES**
**CHAD JAMES GROUP**
1200 VILLA PLACE, 411
NASHVILLE, TN 37212
(615) 818-0099
WWW.CHADJAMES.COM

PAGES 218-219
**CHARLES J. NAFIE**
**CHARLES J. NAFIE ARCHITECTS**
30 EAST 60TH STREET, SUITE 905
NEW YORK, NY 10022
(212) 922-9810
WWW.CJNAARCHITECTS.COM

PAGES 68-69
**CHARLOTTE MOSS**
**CHARLOTTE MOSS, LLC.**
24 EAST 71ST STREET, SUITE 3N
NEW YORK, NY 10021
(212) 308-7088
WWW.CHARLOTTEMOSS.COM

PAGES 74-77
**ELLIE CULLMAN & ALYSSA URBAN**
**CULLMAN & KRAVIS, INC.**
790 MADISON AVENUE, SUITE 700
NEW YORK, NY 10065
(212) 249-3874
WWW.CULLMANKRAVIS.COM

PAGES 118-119
**DARRIN VARDEN**
**DARRIN VARDEN DESIGN**
1831 MADISON AVENUE
NEW YORK, NY 10035
(212) 831-9331
WWW.DARRINVARDENDESIGN.COM

PAGE 2, 124-125, 184-185
**GUILLAUME GENTET**
**DÉCOR BY GUILLAUME GENTET, INC.**
139 FULTON STREET, SUITE 507
NEW YORK, NY 10038
(212) 571-1040
WWW.GUILLAUMEGENTET.COM

PAGES 168-169
**DONNA LIVINGSTON**
**DONNA LIVINGSTON DESIGN**
8811 ALDEN DRIVE, SUITE 2
LOS ANGELES, CA 90048
(310) 273-1855
WWW.DLIVINGSTONDESIGN.COM

# THE DESIGNERS

PAGES 122-123
**DREW McGUKIN**
**DREW McGUKIN INTERIORS**
154 WEST 27TH STREET, SUITE 5E
NEW YORK, NY 10001
(212) 366-5332
WWW.DREWMCGUKIN.COM

PAGES 212-213
**HARRY HEISSMANN**
**HARRY HEISSMANN, INC.**
545 WEST 45TH STREET, SUITE 1104
NEW YORK, NY 10036
(212) 586-0600
WWW.HARRYHEISSMANNINC.COM

PAGES 28-29
**ANTHONY INGRAO & RANDY KEMPER**
**INGRAO, INC.**
17 EAST 64TH STREET
NEW YORK, NY 10065
(212) 472-5400
WWW.INGRAOINC.COM

PAGES 156-157
**JOLIE KOREK**
**JOLIE KOREK & CO.**
15 CAMPDEN ROAD
SCARSDALE, NY 10583
(914) 329-2990
WWW.JOLIEKOREK.COM

PAGES 94-95
**EILEEN KATHRYN BOYD**
**EILEEN KATHRYN BOYD INTERIORS**
251 MAIN STREET
HUNTINGTON, NY 11743
(631) 427-6400
WWW.EKBINTERIORS.COM

PAGES 142-143
**PATRICIA HEALING AND DANIEL BARSANTI**
**HB HOME**
NEW YORK, GREENWICH, AND WESTPORT
(646) 837-6422
WWW.HBHOME.COM

PAGES 70-71, 186-187
**INSON WOOD**
**INSON DUBOIS WOOD, LLC.**
31 WEST 27TH STREET, 10D
NEW YORK, NY 10001
(212) 343-1177
WWW.INSONWOOD.COM

PAGES 228-229
**JOYCE SILVERMAN**
**JOYCE D. SILVERMAN INTERIORS**
BROOKLYN, NY
(718) 336-4386
WWW.JOYSLIVA.COM

PAGES 188-189
**ELIZABETH BOLOGNINO**
**ELIZABETH BOLOGNINO INTERIORS, LLC.**
34 NORTH 7TH STREET, SUITE 10F
BROOKLYN, NY 11249
(718) 599-2782
WWW.ELIZABETHBOLOGNINO.COM

PAGES 192-193
**JAMES HUNIFORD**
**HUNIFORD DESIGN STUDIO**
210 11TH AVENUE, 610
NEW YORK, NY 10001
(212) 717-9177
WWW.HUNIFORD.COM

PAGES 112-113
**JENNIFER COHLER MASON**
**J. COHLER MASON DESIGN**
23 EAST 67TH STREET, SUITE 9C
NEW YORK, NY 10065
(212) 418-1230
WWW.JCOHLERMASON.COM

PAGES 132-133
**JUSTIN SHAULIS**
**JUSTIN SHAULIS, INC.**
105 WEST 55TH STREET, 5D
NEW YORK, NY 10065
(917) 592-9308
WWW.JUSTINSHAULIS.COM

PAGES 58-59, 78-79
**ERIC COHLER**
**ERIC COHLER DESIGN**
95 FIFTH AVENUE
NEW YORK, NY 10003
(212) 737-8600
WWW.ERICCOHLERDESIGN.COM

PAGES 128-129
**TRICIA HUNTLEY**
**HUNTLEY & CO. INTERIOR DESIGN**
1655 45TH STREET
WASHINGTON, DC 20007
(202) 462-3030
WWW.HUNTLEYANDCOMPANY.COM

PAGES 202-203
**JAIME WALTERS**
**JAIME WALTERS**
(917) 780-2161
WWW.JAIMEWALTERS.COM

PAGES 42-43
**RICHARD CERRONE, RHONDA ELEISH & LISA HYMAN**
**LILLIAN AUGUST**
32 KNIGHT STREET
NORWALK, CT 06851
(204) 847-1596
WWW.LILLIANAUGUST.COM

PAGES 80-81
**GARY McBOURNIE**
**GARY McBOURNIE, INC.**
71 NEWBURY STREET, SUITE 300
BOSTON, MA 02116
(617) 542-5700
WWW.GMCBINC.COM

PAGE 8, 13, 196-197
**IRIS DANKNER**
**ID CREATIONS**
524 EAST 72ND STREET, 32C
NEW YORK, NY 10021
(917) 855-5944
WWW.HOLIDAYHOUSEDESIGNSHOW.COM

PAGES 30-31, 84-85
**JAMES RIXNER**
**JAMES RIXNER, INC.**
121 MORTON STREET, SUITE 4B
NEW YORK, NY 10014
(212) 206-7439
WWW.JAMESRIXNER.COM

PAGES 144-147, 176-179
**JENNIFER MABLEY & AUSTIN HANDLER**
**MABLEY HANDLER INTERIOR DESIGN**
34 HEAD OF POND ROAD
WATER MILL, NY 11976
(631) 726-7300
WWW.MABLEYHANDLER.COM

# THE DESIGNERS

PAGES 140-141
**SCOTT MADDUX & JO LEGLEUD**
**MADDUX CREATIVE**
44(0)20 8265 8153
WWW.MADDUXCREATIVE.COM

PAGES 88-89
**MICHAEL TAVANO**
**MICHAEL TAVANO DESIGN**
2201 3RD AVENUE
NEW YORK, NY 10035
(212) 564-0034
WWW.MICHAELTAVANO.COM

PAGES 216-217
**PATRICK MCGRATH**
**PATRICK MCGRATH DESIGN**
880 FIFTH AVENUE, 10A
NEW YORK, NY 10021
(917) 971-7970
WWW.PATRICKMCGRATHDESIGN.COM

PAGES 108-111
**SUZANNE EASON**
**PLUMRIDGEHOUSE I SUZANNE EASON**
107 PARSONAGE ROAD
GREENWICH, CT 06830
(917) 907-4205
WWW.SUZANNEEASON.COM

PAGES 180-181
**MARSHALL WATSON**
**MARSHALL WATSON INTERIORS**
105 WEST 72ND STREET, SUITE 9B
NEW YORK, NY 10023
(212) 595-5995
WWW.MARSHALLWATSONINTERIORS.COM

PAGES 102-103
**PAMELA BANKER**
**PAMELA BANKER ASSOCIATES**
136 EAST 57TH STREET
NEW YORK, NY 10022
(212) 308-5030
WWW.PAMELABANKER.COM

PAGES 44-45
**PATRIK LÖNN**
**PATRIK LÖNN DESIGN**
12 DEBROSSES STREET, 2ND FLOOR
NEW YORK, NY 10013
(212) 400-4841
WWW.PATRIKLONN.COM

PAGES 100-101
**RACHEL LAXER**
**RACHEL LAXER INTERIORS**
10A HEATHCOTE ROAD
SCARSDALE, NY 10583
(914) 621-8515
WWW.RLAXERINTERIORS.COM

PAGES 62-65
**MATTHEW PATRICK SMYTH**
**MATTHEW PATRICK SMYTH, INC.**
136 EAST 57TH STREET, 901
NEW YORK, NY 10022
(212) 333-5353
WWW.MATTHEWSMYTH.COM

PAGES 66-67
**PARIS FORINO**
**PARIS FORINO DESIGN**
210 WEST 29TH STREET, 4TH FLOOR
NEW YORK, NY 10001
(212) 601-9359
WWW.PARISFORINODESIGN.COM

PAGES 18-21
**PAULA CARAVELLI**
**PAULA + MARTHA, LLC.**
200 CENTRAL PARK SOUTH, 35C
NEW YORK, NY 10019
(917) 267-3405
WWW.PAULAMARTHA.COM

PAGES 224-225
**RENA CHERNY**
**RC STUDIO**
WWW.RENACHERNYSTUDIO.COM

PAGES 160-163
**MELANIE ROY**
**MELANIE ROY DESIGN**
1010 FIFTH AVENUE, 1D
NEW YORK, NY 10028
(917) 446-5651
WWW.MELANIEROYDESIGN.COM

PAGE 6, 114-115
**PATRICK J. HAMILTON**
**PATRICK JAMES HAMILTON DESIGNS**
(646) 645-7071
WWW.ASKPATRICK.BLOGSPOT.COM

PAGES 48-51
**CHARLES PAVARINI III**
**PAVARINI DESIGN**
NEW YORK, NY
(212) 749-2047
WWW.PAVARINIDESIGN.COM

PAGES 174-175
**RICHARD MISHAAN**
**RICHARD MISHAAN DESIGN**
145 HUDSON STREET, SUITE 5A
NEW YORK, NY 10013
(212) 223-7502
WWW.RICHARDMISHAAN.COM

# THE DESIGNERS

PAGE 253
**RIO HAMILTON**
(646) 246-7777
WWW.RIOHAMILTON.COM

PAGES 182-183
**TAMARA MAGEL**
**TAMARA MAGEL**
51 DIVISION STREET
SAG HARBOR, NY 11963
(917) 628-0868
WWW.TAMARAMAGEL.COM

PAGES 82-83
**TOBI FAIRLEY**
**TOBI FAIRLEY INTERIOR DESIGN**
5507 RANCH DRIVE, SUITE 103
LITTLE ROCK, AR 72223
WWW.TOBIFAIRLEY.COM

PAGES 120-121
**AMIE WEITZMAN & MICHAEL HALPERN**
**WEITZMAN HALPERN INTERIOR DESIGN**
52 EAST 76TH STREET
NEW YORK, NY 10021
(212) 249-7666
WWW.WEITZMANHALPERN.COM

PAGES 38-41
**ROBERT PASSAL**
**ROBERT PASSAL INTERIOR & ARCHITECTURAL DESIGN**
333 PARK AVENUE SOUTH, SUITE 4A
NEW YORK, NY 10010
(212) 242-5508
WWW.ROBERTPASSAL.COM

PAGES 170-173
**THOM FILICIA**
**THOM FILICIA, INC.**
200 LEXINGTON AVENUE, SUITE 815
NEW YORK, NY 10016
(212) 736-6454
WWW.THOMFILICIA.COM

PAGES 152-153
**JAYNE MICHAELS AND JOAN MICHAELS**
**2 MICHAELS DESIGN**
360 CENTRAL PARK WEST
NEW YORK, NY 10025
(212) 662-5358
WWW.2MICHAELSDESIGN.COM

PAGES 158-159
**WESLEY MOON**
**WESLEY MOON, INC.**
195 CHRYSTIE STREET, 301
NEW YORK, NY 10002
(212) 785-0392
WWW.WESLEYMOON.COM

PAGES 226-227
**RYAN KORBAN**
WWW.RYANKORBAN.COM

PAGES 154-155
**TIMOTHY BROWN**
**TIMOTHY BROWN STUDIO**
200 LEXINGTON AVE, SUITE 1608
NEW YORK, NY 10016
(212) 255-4895
WWW.TIMOTHYBROWNSTUDIO.COM

PAGE 249
**FREDERICO AZEVEDO**
**UNLIMITED EARTH CARE, INC.**
P.O. BOX 3178
SAG HARBOR, NY 11963
(631) 445-2046
WWW.UNLIMITEDEARTHCARE.COM

PAGES 22-23
**MATTHEW WHITE & FRANK WEBB**
**WHITE WEBB, LLC.**
105 EAST 34TH STREET, 116
NEW YORK, NY 10016
(212) 889-2900
WWW.WHITEWEBB.COM

PAGES 204-205
**SASHA BIKOFF**
**SASHA BIKOFF INTERIOR DESIGN**
(917) 439-2435
WWW.SASHABIKOFF.COM

PAGES 220-223
**TINA RAMCHANDANI**
**TINA RAMCHANDANI CREATIVE**
70 EAST 10TH STREET, 7P
NEW YORK, NY 10003
(212) 321-0037
WWW.TINARAMCHANDANI.COM

PAGES 96-97, 134-135
**VICENTE WOLF**
**VICENTE WOLF ASSOCIATES, INC.**
333 WEST 39TH STREET, 10TH FLOOR
NEW YORK, NY 10018
(212) 244-5008
WWW.VICENTEWOLF.COM

# SOURCES

## FRONT MATTER

**OPPOSITE TITLE PAGE**
**DÉCOR BY GUILLAUME GENTET, INC.**
**2013—WOMEN'S DAY CAFE**

Sconces: www.baccarat.com

Steel palm tree planters: www.authenticprovence.com

Paint: www.benjaminmoore.com

Furniture: www.brownjordan.com

Silver serving trays: www.christofle.com

Mohair main fabric and confidante sofa: www.christopherhyland.com

Pillow fabric: www.creations-metaphores.com

Custom café tables and wrought-iron base: www.glacseat.com

Vases: www.globalviews.com

Trim for sofa and tent fabric: www.kravet.com

Tent trim and perimeter drapery fabric: www.leejofa.com

Chair seat fabric: www.lelievre.eu

Banquette: www.leonardosupholstery.com

Café chair fabric: www.brunschwig.com

Rug: www.starkcarpet.com

Trim: www.samuelandsons.com

Design for central confidante sofa and bar and trellis design: Guillaume Gentet

Trellis and perimeter through planters: Woodland Remodeling & Cabinetry

**OPPOSITE CONTENTS**
**BITTT GROUP**
**2011—THE BIRTHDAY CELEBRATION**

Chrome cart and ice bucket: www.1stdibs.com

Curtains: www.anthonylawrence.com

Paint: www.benjaminmoore.com

Desk: www.bungalow5.com

Light fixture: www.clsterling.com

Carpet: www.fortstreetstudio.com

**PAGE 6**
**PATRICK JAMES HAMILTON DESIGNS**
**2013—ST. PATRICK'S DAY**

Window treatment: www.anthonylawrence.com

Artwork: www.danielcooneyfineart.com

Frame: www.jpocker.com

Barware: www.waterford.com

Metal sculpture: www.johnlyledesign.com

**PAGE 8**
**ID CREATIONS**
**2014—BUNGALOW**

Rug: www.fjhakimian.com

Accessories: www.vicentewolf.com

Console: www.ercole.com

Artwork: www.dorfmanprojects.com

End table: www.lorinmarsh.com

Light fixture: www.interieurs.com

Sofa: www.ef-lm.com

Coffee table: www.nancycorzine.com

Pillows: www.biasicatani.com

**PAGE 13**
**ID CREATIONS**
**2014—BRIDAL SUITE**

Curtains: www.dedar.com

Mirror/TV: www.audiodoctor.com

Chair: www.ef-lm.com

Accessories: www.lunareshome.com; www.michaelcfina.com

Rug: www.starkcarpet.com

Wall covering: www.mayaromanoff.com

Lighting: www.ochre.net

Artwork: www.christinawatka.com

Curtain fabrication: www.yourhomestore.com

## ACADEMY MANSION THE ENTRANCE FOYER

**PAGES 18–21**
**PAULA + MARTHA, LLC.**
**2012—WINTER SOLSTICE**

Custom framing: www.jpocker.com

Jacques Jarrige Fiori Chandelier, Eric Schmitt vase, Jacques Jarrige sculpture screen, floor lamps, Cristina Salusti gold interior bowls and sconces: www.valeriegoodmangallery.com

Custom print (Evelyn H. Lauder by Douglas Friedman for *Harper's Bazaar*): www.duggal.com

Antique settee: www.b4decor.com

Agostini dining chairs and Brancusi parchment stools: www.tomthomasgallery.com

Ribbon rug by Paula Caravelli and silk area rug by Paula Caravelli: www.dorislieslieblau.com

Bronze floor lamps, patinated bronze sconces by Hervé van der Straeten, Marc Bankowsky, and Miguel Cisterna, bench, seven ceramic architectural elements, and ceramic table lamp: www.maisongerard.com

Leather console: www.geraldblandinc.com

Flowers: www.lolivier.com

Paintings by Ron Salome Gorchov 2012 and Dinah 2012: www.cheimread.com

Baccarat 1940s crystal chandelier, Alfred Hendricks armchairs, and Constantin: www.tomthomasgallery.com

Torchières: www.miriamellner.com

Custom sofa: www.paulamartha.com

French steel center table: www.briggshouse.com

Lucite chair, 1960s: www.glendooley.com

Nada Debs coffee table: www.21stgallery.com

Neoclassical-style pine urns and African bench: www.geraldblandinc.com

Custom pillow and drapery fabrication: www.pillowsetplus.com

Drapery fabrics: www.joann.com

Sofa and pillow fabrics: www.cowtan.com

Table skirt fabric: www.knoll.com/textiles

Fur throw: www.hollandandsherry.com

Framing: www.jpocker.com

**PAGES 22–23**
**WHITE WEBB, LLC.**
**2015—LOVING DAY**

Fabrics, Giselle settee, consoles, and side chairs: www.donghia.com

Horn sconce: www.circalighting.com

Armchair, ottoman, and artwork: www.whitewebb.com

Folding screens tape-embroidered border: www.samuelandsons.com

Orb lamps: www.ylighting.com

Artwork: www.lilacgallerynyc.com; www.dillongallery.com; www.cherylhazan.com

Statue: www.sabinhoward.com

Glass accessories: www.seguso.com

Custom sculpture pedestal: www.ipaintandcontract.com

## ACADEMY MANSION THE PARLOR

**PAGES 26–27**
**GEOFFREY BRADFIELD, INC.**
**2012—REMEMBRANCE OF THINGS PAST**

Rugs: www.starkcarpet.com; www.kylebunting.com

Wall covering: www.astekwallcovering.com

Sconces: www.lladro.com

Antiques: www.johnsalibello.com; www.newel.com

Louise Nevelson artwork: www.nohrahaimegallery.com

Acrylic furniture: www.interiorsbyroyale.com

Fabric on pillows: www.christopherhyland.com; www.jrobertscott.com

Chandelier: www.johnsalibello.com

**PAGES 28-29**
**INGRAO, INC.**
**2013—CASABLANCA CHRISTMAS**

Furniture: www.fendi.com

Pillow fabrics: www.dedar.com

Mirrors: www.mirrorfair.com

Curtains: www.nylaregence.com

Chandelier and sconces: www.cosulichinteriors.com; www.newel.com

Accessories: www.us.christofle.com

Piano: www.steinway.com

Parchment: www.newel.com

Rugs: www.fjhakimian.com

# SOURCES

**PAGES 30–31**
**JAMES RIXNER, INC.**
**2015—SAINT ANDREW'S DAY**

Gulliver chair, Taylor sectional, little bud chair, and Liv daybed: www.crlaine.com

Cocktail table, Fenimore chair, Zelda occasional tables, Ingalls desk, console, and Hayford dresser: www.ejvictor.com

Grosvenor lamp, billow chest, and enclosure pedestal: www.theodorealexander.com

Barocco console: www.colombomobili.com

Tura bar cabinet: www.lorinmarsh.com

Boxwell tables: www.curreycodealers.com

Chandelier and sconces: www.saint-louis.com

Fabric: www.hollandandsherry.com

Trim: www.samuelandsons.com

Rug: www.tufenkiancarpets.com

**PAGES 32–33**
**AMY LAU DESIGN**
**2014—WINTER WONDERLAND CELEBRATION: BACCARAT'S 250TH ANNIVERSARY**

Mirror glass and installation: www.manhattanshade.com

Contracting: www.donadic.com

Window treatments: www.erikbruce.com

Custom hide rugs: www.kylebunting.com

Decorative painting: www.fieldfinish.com

Furniture: www.maisongerard.com

Fabric: www.dedar.com

Florist: www.vanvlietandtrap.com

Upholstery: www.dune-ny.com

**PAGES 34–35**
**ALLY COULTER DESIGNS**
**2011—MOTHER'S DAY**

Furniture and accessories: www.ralphlaurenhome.com

Rug: www.starkcarpet.com

Piano: www.steinway.com

Photography: www.shellibreidenbach.com

Artwork: www.farber.com; www.staleywise.com

Accessories: www.lorinmarsh.com

Antique furniture and accessories: www.trianonantiques.com; www.davidduncanantiques.com; www.nicholasbrawer.com

Woodwork: www.hyde-park.com

Window treatments: www.martinalbert.com

## ACADEMY MANSION THE LIBRARY

**PAGES 38–41**
**ROBERT PASSAL INTERIOR & ARCHITECTURAL DESIGN**
**2015—BOXING DAY**

Pillows: www.hollandandsherry.com

Chandelier: www.ziapriven.com

Rug: www.starkcarpet.com

Sofa and lounge chair: www.nycustomfurnishings

Sofa fabric, lounge chair fabric, chair-seat fabric, and pillow fabric: www.rondacarman.com

Bolster pillow fabrics, gray throw on sofa, plaid throw, and chair-seat fabric: www.johnstonscashmere.com

Ceramic stools: www.emissaryusa.com

Artwork and gold object on table: www.voltzclarke.com

Floor lamps flanking sofa, Hochstetler lighting, desk lamp behind sofa, vintage brass cantilevered casella desk lamp, desk chair behind sofa, chest to right of mantel, and armchair: www.leecalicchioltd.com

Coffee table: www.newel.com

Table beside lounge chair: www.johnrosselli.com

Dining chairs, vintage Robsjohn-Gibbings, and table with dining chair: www.reaganhayes.com

Console table: www.aerin.com

Ice bucket and decanters: www.richardcohencollection.com

**PAGES 42–43**
**LILLIAN AUGUST**
**2014—CELEBRATION OF THE HOLIDAYS**

Fabrics and accessories: www.hollandandsherry.com

Furnishings and design: www.lillianaugust.com

Upholstery: www.hickorywhite.com

Drapery trim: www.samuelandsons.com

Sisal: www.fibreworks.com

Chandelier: www.evbantiques.com

Fine art: www.arcaturefineart.com

Window hardware: www.morgik.com

Twisted juniper console: www.aretecollection.com

Antique tabriz rug: www.fjhakimian.com

Crystal accessories: www.baccarat.com

Alpaca throw: www.hollandandsherry.com

**PAGES 44–45**
**PATRIK LÖNN DESIGN**
**2013—A SWEDE IN SCOTTISH HOLIDAY SPIRIT**

Rug: www.fjhakimian.com

Eglomise walls: www.vbricelj.com

Painter: www.jpeckpainting.com

Throw blankets: www.johnstonscashmere.com; www.calzeat.com

Upholstery fabrics: www.islemill.com; www.macnaughton-group.com; www.nycustomfurnishings.com; www.beggandcompany.com

Fireplace screen and tools: www.wmhjacksoncompany.com

Flowers and arrangements: www.lolivier.com

Panels for the eglomise paint: www.capitolglassnyc.com

Upholstered ceiling: Albert Vitiello Decorators Workroom

Decorative silver: www.hamiltonandinches.com

Candles: www.shearer-candles.com

## ACADEMY MANSION THE DINING ROOM

**PAGES 48–51**
**PAVARINI DESIGN**
**2008—HAPPY THANKSGIVING**

Window treatments: www.windowworks-nj.com

Fabrics and trimmings: www.stroheim.com

Passementerie: www.samuelandsons.com

Furniture and artwork: www.rolandantiques.com; www.agostinoantiques.com; www.hydeparkantiques.com; www.davidduncanantiques.com; Universe Antiques, Inc.

Wood floor: www.floorworksny.com

Accessories: www.lorinmarsh.com

Exterior landscaping: www.ldgn-ny.com

Custom lampshades: www.orientallampshade.com

Crystal and china: www.baccarat.com; www.lalique.com; www.michaelcfina.com; www.bernardaud.com; www.thewineenthusiast.com

Cove lighting technology: www.levylighting.com

Table linens: www.anichini.com; www.casadelbianco.com

Artwork: www.spaniermanmodern.com; Richmond Burton

Flowers: www.lexingtonflowershop.com

**PAGES 52–53**
**BJÖRN BJÖRNSSON INTERIOR DESIGN, LLC.**
**2015—FROZEN**

Birch winter wonderland trees: www.restorationhardware.com

Nicole lamps and Jasper lanterns: www.arteriors.com

Sablier chair, Portico fixture, Jensen mirror, La Pausa chair, Harper console, Tatler side table, Bizet side table, Chez cabinet, and Martigny sofa: www.christopherguy.com

Crystal logs and decorative pillows on side chair: www.kravet.com

Rug: www.starkcarpet.com

Clover tray, Heliopolis uplights, large star andirons, Lucretius side table, and Lyell pedestal tables: www.johnlyledesign.com

Galaxy console and Galaxy pedestal: www.interiorsbyroyale.com

Ice crystals: www.jamaligarden.com

Floating illuminated balls: www.amazon.com

Paintings: "Above and Beyond," "Untitled," and "Untitled": www.hannaseiman.com

# SOURCES

**PAGES 54–55**
**ALLY COULTER DESIGNS**
**2014—A ROMAN HOLIDAY**

Books: www.assouline.com

Furniture and accessories: www.fendi.com; www.dakotajackson.com

Antique accessories: www.newel.com

Artwork: www.dutchpaintings.com; www.metamorfaux-decorative-painting.com; www.robertofernandez.com; www.farber.com

Furniture: www.ralphlaurenhome.com

Rug: www.starkcarpet.com

Wall covering: www.mayaromanoff.com

Fabric: www.dedar.com

Crystal accessories: www.baccarat.com

Window treatments: www.martinalbert.com

Piano: www.steinway.com

## ACADEMY MANSION THE MASTER BEDROOM

**PAGES 58–59**
**ERIC COHLER DESIGN**
**2009—FATHER'S DAY STUDY**

Construction: www.fanuka.com

Floor preparation: www.professionaldesignflooring.com

Venetian plaster and painting: www.abpaintingservices.ca

Hand-painted floor: Dean Barger Studios

Ceiling: Couture Interiors

Windows and upholstery: www.windowswallsandmore.com

Window seats: www.democustom.com

Ceiling wallpaper: www.ralphlaurenhome.com

Lighting: www.circalighting.com

Hand-painted pillows: www.timothybrownstudio.com

Sisal carpet: www.beauvaiscarpets.com

Pool table: www.blattbilliards.com

Slipper chairs: www.billybaldwinstudio.com/index.html

Desk: www.lizobrien.com

Leather desk chair: www.knoll.com

Bar stools: www.dessinfournir.com

Cabinet lamps: www.karlkemp.com

Walnut holland cabinet: www.romanthomas.com

Linen settee fabric: www.donghia.com

Black pony hair: www.edelmanleather.com

Fireplace stools: www.wmhjacksoncompany.com

Lampshades: www.bhonbhon.com

Frames: Jinpra NY

Metal racecar: www.bizarrebazaarltd.com

Flowers: SMR Design Inc.

Rush log basket: Mallett Antiques

Art piece on mantel: Andrew Huston

Art installation: www.platypusfineart.com

**PAGES 60–61**
**CAMPION PLATT INTERIORS**
**2013—DREAM**

Rugs: Carini Lang

Furniture: www.sleepstudio.com; www.giorgettiusa.com

Window treatments: David Michael Interiors

Fabric: www.calvinfabrics.com; www.donghia.com

Contractor: www.fanuka.com

Carpet: www.starkcarpet.com

Artwork: www.richardtaittinger.com; Sergio Manzari

**PAGES 62–65**
**MATTHEW PATRICK SMYTH, INC.**
**2014—ANNIVERSARY ROOM**

All fabrics and "Maria" trim: www.fschumacher.com

Carpet: www.pattersonflynnmartin.com

Window treatments, Givenchy sofa, pair of Bridgewater chairs, upholstery of antique chairs, and pillows: www.anthonylawrence.com

Pair of regency consoles, Charles X clock, and sculpture by Curtis Jere: www.florianpapp.com

Regency mahogany sofa and 19th century English screen: www.leecalicchioltd.com

Pair of cast-bronze sheep and pair of English regency chairs: www.davidduncanantiques.com

Brompton coffee table and French bronze globe chandelier: www.luccaantiques.com

English Regency center table: www.sutterantiques.com

Pair of brass faux-bamboo tables and pair of square brass tables: www.1stdibs.com/dealers/lerebours-antiques/

Collage by Robert Courtright: www.pavelzoubok.com

"Night Fishing" by Emilia Dubicki: www.giampietrogallery.com

"Whitewater" by Victor-Raul Garcia: www.victorraulgarcia.com

"Rodin-Balzac" by Gerald Incandela: www.geraldincandela.com

Miscellaneous artwork: bronze vase by Anasthasia Millot, pair of "Photophore Candle Lights" by Anasthasia Millot, and pair of andirons in polished bronze by Jacques Jarrige: www.valeriegoodmangallery.com

Miscellaneous accessories: www.michaelaram.com

Spotlight fixtures: www.mskilluminations.com

Pair of pharmacy floor lamps, Paulo floor light, fluted spire table lamps, pair of TriBeCa floor lamps: www.circalighting.com

**PAGES 66–67**
**PARIS FORINO DESIGN**
**2015—HOME FOR THE HOLIDAYS**

All fabrics: www.jimthompsonfabrics.com

Area rug: www.saccocarpet.com

All upholstery, pillows, and window seat cushions: www.dmitriyco.com

Antique tables and antique accessories: www.dmitriyco.com

Chessboard, table lamp, Phare lamp, tea set, vases, dog and cat candles, and hanging mirror: www.ateliercourbet.com

Parchment screen: www.atelierviollet.com

All leathers and Alexander LaMont accessories: www.angelabrownltd.com

All drapery and duvet: Contour Drapery, Inc.

Custom stone coffee table: www.eurasiastone.com

Painting and electrical work: www.copperwoodspecialties.com

Arrow suspension lights: www.apparatusstudio.com

Yassin lamp: www.biancolightspace.com

Deco accessories: www.highstyledeco.com

Ceramic stools: www.thefutureperfect.com

Bench accessories: www.suiteny.com

Trunks and accessories: www.lindahorn.com

All sheets and throw blankets: www.frette.com

Paint: www.farrow-ball.com

**PAGES 68–69**
**CHARLOTTE MOSS, LLC.**
**2012—EVERY DAY IS A HOLIDAY**

Framed art from the Charlotte Moss Collection: www.soicher-marin.com

Fabrics from the Charlotte Moss Collection: www.fabricut.com

Upholstery: www.howardsupholstery.com

Wallpaper and paint contracting: John Fasano

Furniture from the Charlotte Moss Icons Collection: www.centuryfurniture.com

Carpet: www.saccocarpet.com

Carpeting from the Charlotte Moss Collection: www.starkcarpet.com

Accessories: www.mecox.com

**PAGES 70–71**
**INSON DUBOIS WOOD, LLC.**
**2011—CHINESE NEW YEAR**

Koons puppy ceramic vase: www.jeffkoons.com

Dragon pillow fabric, matching custom gold trim, and tieback window treatments: www.christopherhyland.com

All lighting: www.charles.fr

Cashmere throw: www.casadelbianco.com

Pillows: www.donghia.com

# SOURCES

Three-legged table: www.dakotajackson.com

Yellow red diamond painting by Larry Zox and painting over mantel by Ron Ehrlich: www.stephenhallergallery.com

Silk rug: www.orleyshabahang.com

All porcelain other than Koons puppy: www.lladro.com

Ceiling chandelier by Hervé van der Straeten: www.maisongerard.com

Silver egg: www.r-and-company.com

Geometric white paintings: www.michaeldickeyart.com

Mid-century dining chairs: www.vandenakkerantiques.com

Lacquer wall painting: www.nordiccustom.com

Yellow silk hand-painted and embroidered wall paper: www.fromenthal.co.uk

Curtain fabric: www.scalamandre.com

Zebra chair: www.jrobertscott.com

Tray table: www.johnboone.com

Jean Michel Frank table, Puhlmann desk, and gold cabinet: www.pollaro.com

## ACADEMY MANSION
## THE SITTING ROOM

### PAGES 74–77
### CULLMAN & KRAVIS, INC.
### 2013—CELEBRATING 30 YEARS

All upholstery: www.anthonylawrence.com

Window treatments: www.curtainmaker.net

Paint and wallpaper installation: www.wbpaint.com

Wallpaper: www.phillipjeffries.com

White cowhide area rug: www.beauvaiscarpets.com

Sofa and chair fabric: www.cowtan.com

Chaise fabric: www.brunschwig.com

Lumbar pillow fabric: www.lesageinterieurs.com

Roman shade and throw pillow fabric: www.prestigious.co.uk/en/

Antique sideboard, drink table, and pair of benches: www.bgoecklerantiques.com

Antique vitrine, cabinets, armchairs, and accessories: www.karlkemp.com

Antique coffee table and desk: www.hmluther.com

Antique chaise and accessories: www.johnsalibello.com

Crystal lamps and decorative objects: www.phoenixgalleryny.com

Antique sconces and obelisks: www.newel.com

Antique light fixtures and candlesticks: www.delapuenteantiques.com

Antique Lucite lamps: www.mallettbuildings.com

Fur throw: www.frette.com

Antique orange vases: www.florianpapp.com

All art: www.ruthcatone.com

Lampshades: www.mgabareelampshades.com

Picture frames: www.williamyeowardcrystal.com

Black boxes: www.alexantiques.com

Pair of mirrors and frame on painting over the mantel: www.lowy1907.com

Cake stand: www.larreastudio.com

Candlesticks and bronze tray: www.maisongerard.com

### PAGES 78–79
### ERIC COHLER DESIGN
### 2010—MOTHER'S DAY

Settee: www.antonytodd.com

Wallpaper installation: Couture Interiors

Fabric: www.creationbaumann.com

Chair: www.dwr.com

Console: www.karlkemp.com

Dining chairs: Ex Collection Jayne Wrightsman

China and accessories: www.barneys.com

Stemware: www.scullyandscully.com

Window-treatment fabric: www.fschumacher.com

Contractor: www.fanuka.com

Mirrors: Guy Regal, Ltd.

Dining chair back fabric: www.hollyhunt.com

Chandeliers and sconces: www.johnsalibello.com

Dining chair fabric by Eric Cohler: www.leejofa.com

Topiaries: www.lexingtongardens.com

Dining table: www.malmaison.com

Ceiling wallpaper: www.phillipjeffries.com

Artwork: www.spaniermanmodern.com

Rugs: www.starkcarpet.com

Coffee table: Couture Showrooms

Fireplace screen and accessories: www.wmhjacksoncompany.com

Window treatments and upholstery: www.windowsandwalls.com

Calligraphy: Wade Hampton

Solar shades: www.manhattanshade.com

Painting: MPC Painting

Floor lamp: www.ef-lm.com

### PAGES 80–81
### GARY McBOURNIE, INC.
### 2014—CARIBBEAN ISLAND HOLIDAY

Fabric for tenting and pillows: www.antillesdesigns.com

Fabrication of tent: www.jonasworkroom.com

Mirrors over doors and fireplace: www.mirrorfair.com

Bamboo blinds: www.backbayshutter.com

Jute rug: www.meridastudio.com

Chandelier: www.lizobrien.com

Sofas: www.gmcbinc.com

Fabrication of pillows: www.jonasworkroom.com

Fabric on sofa: www.glant.com

John Hutton chairs and benches: www.neostudiosnyc.com

Cocktail table: www.gmcbinc.com

Pair of neoclassic-design standing lamps: www.davidduncanantiques.com

Pair of glazed table lamps: www.johnbooneinc.com

Lampshades: www.blanchefield.com

Teak sideboard: www.horsemanantiques.net

Barware: www.marymahoney.com

Fabrics and trims: www.samuelandsons.com

Abstract painting: "Of Song and Blossom" by Michael Rich: www.oldspoutergallery.com

Set of framed parrot prints: www.lussierlajoieframing.com

Sofa table bases: www.neostudiosnyc.com

Glass for sofa table: www.mirrorfair.com

Bamboo étagères: www.sjulian.1stdibs.com

### PAGES 82–83
### TOBI FAIRLEY INTERIOR DESIGN
### 2012—SPRING FORWARD

Hickory chair: www.hickorychair.com

Wall covering: www.phillipjeffries.com

Sconces: www.dunesandduchess.com

Lamps: www.swanklighting.com

Fabrics: www.duralee.com; www.fschumacher.com

Embroidery on drapery: www.villasavoia.us

### PAGES 84–85
### JAMES RIXNER, INC.
### 2011—VALENTINE'S DAY

Sofa, accent table, chairs, mirrors, drawer chests, and floor lamp: www.centuryfurniture.com

Cocktail table: www.lorinmarsh.com

Rug: www.tibetano.com

Chandeliers: www.foundrylighting.com

Vintage Sconces: www.chameleon59.com

## ACADEMY MANSION
## THE FRONT BEDROOM

### PAGES 88–89
### MICHAEL TAVANO DESIGN
### 2014—LA FÊTE NATIONALE

Lighting: www.baroncelli.com

Fabric: www.jab.de/en

Art: www.waterfallmansion.com

All furniture: www.roche-bobois.com

Paint: www.farrow-ball.com

Flooring: www.alphaworkshops.org

# SOURCES

Window treatments and fabrication: www.marksandtavano.com

Construction: Max Construction

**PAGES 90–91**
**BARBARA OSTROM & ASSOCIATES**
**2008—MOTHER'S DAY**

Carpet: www.starkcarpet.com

Artwork: www.acagalleries.com; www.danielleannmillican.com

Chinese vases and accessories: www.ark-antiques.com

Drapery, duvet, and throw pillows: Baum Drapery Workroom

Fabric: www.brunschwig.com

Bedding: www.casadelbianco.com

Accessories and pillows: www.davidduncanantiques.com

Accessories: www.englishcountry-antiques.blogspot.com; www.hydeparkantiques.com; www.newel.com; www.waterford.com

Mural over fireplace: www.dianewarnermurals.com

Desk: www.ebanista.com

Light fixtures: www.hinsonlighting.com

Upholstery: Julia Gray

Coffee table: www.lorinmarsh.com

Custom sofa: www.mason-art.com

Mirrored tables: www.nancycorzine.com

Accessories and night tables: Nicholas Antiques

Paint: www.pantone.com

Plants: Roger Wohrle

Trimming: www.samuelandsons.com

Flower arrangements: The Secret Garden

**PAGES 92–93**
**ANTONINO BUZZETTA DESIGN**
**2015—MOTHER'S DAY**

Custom vinyl floor tiles: www.mirthstudio.com

Custom area rug: www.edwardfields.com

Vincent sofa, sectional sofa, club chairs, set of three pedestals, occasional chairs, fois bois, desk, mirror, pair of chandeliers, black and white rose on white linen, sectional fabric, sofa fabric, and black hide pillow: www.bradley-usa.com

Cocktail table: www.studiovandenakker.com

Pair of Chelsea lamps: www.kathrynmccoydesigns.com

Ultraviolet pillow and smoked quartz pillow: www.romo.com

"Hollywood in Beverly Blue": www.donghia.com

**PAGES 94–95**
**EILEEN KATHRYN BOYD INTERIORS**
**2011—SUNDAY IN REPOSE**

Custom tufted cube ottoman, custom Parsons table for ottoman, vintage wood side table, artwork, zebra ottoman, vintage console, French chairs, French carved corner chair, round draped table with linen topper, and accessories: www.ekbinteriors.com

Leopard throw: www.dorianbahr.com

Grasscloth topper for carved console: www.phillipjeffries.com

Vase, barware, and candlesticks on mantel: Rogaska America, Inc.

White table lamps and murano glass–purple lamps: www.arteriorshome.com

Paint: www.benjaminmoore.com

Custom wall murals: www.blackcrowstudios.com

Upholstery: Cesar Molina Upholstery

Floor lamps, hanging lantern, and wall sconces: www.circalighting.com

Fabric: www.duralee.com; www.fschumacher.com; www.romo.com

Teapot and china: www.richardginori1735usa.com

Sofa, white wood framed chair, oval ottoman, taupe upholstered chair, and square lamp table: www.henredon.com

Trim on sofa: www.houles.com

Artwork: www.kerryirvinefineart.com; www.lostcityarts.com

Living room carpet: www.maslandcarpets.com

Boxwoods: www.scarsellasflorist.com

Fabric for blue chair and fabric for taupe chair: www.sunbrella.com

**PAGES 96–97**
**VICENTE WOLF ASSOCIATES, INC.**
**2012—SWEDISH WINTER DREAM ROOM**

Furniture and accessories: www.vicentewolf.com; www.anthonylawrence.com

Painter: Sylvie of Metamorfaux

Furniture: www.centuryfurniture.com

Fabrics: www.brunschwig.com

## ACADEMY MANSION THE HOME OFFICE

**PAGES 100–101**
**RACHEL LAXER INTERIORS**
**2013—VALENTINE'S DAY**

Fur throw: www.pologeorgis.com

Fabric, sofa fabric, and throw cushions: www.pierrefrey.com

Wallpaper: www.phillipjeffries.com

Decorative vases: www.lladro.com; www.robertkuo.com

Wallpaper installation: www.ljkfinishes.com

Antique mirror: www.leecalicchioltd.com

Ceiling light: www.clsterling.com

Drapery workroom: www.blindtekdesignersystems.com

Paint: www.benjaminmoore.com

Curtain fabric: www.carolynray.com

Moving company: www.airseapacking.com

Side tables: www.valeriegoodmangallery.com

Artwork: www.dinagoldstein.com

Chairs by Mattia Bonetti: www.paulkasmingallery.com

Coffee tables by Peter Dayton and Ray Geary: www.thegreyarea.com

Photography by Raul Higuera: www.veredart.com

**PAGES 102–103**
**PAMELA BANKER ASSOCIATES**
**2014—NEW YEAR'S EVE AT HOME**

New carpeting: www.beauvaiscarpets.com

Game table: www.fairtlough.com

Painting services: www.sammysinteriorpaint.com

Upholstery and drapery: www.versaillesdrapery.com

Table accessories: www.empiredelicious.com

Fabric for upholstery: www.peterfasano.com

Bench: www.tuckerrobbins.com

Wallpaper: www.clarencehouse.com

Backgammon board: www.gldecorativefinishes.com

**PAGES 104–105**
**ASHLEY DARRYL**
**2015—FATHER'S DAY**

Wallpaper: www.phillipjeffries.com

Paint: www.farrow-ball.com

Valence: www.hollandsherry.com

Curtain panels: www.fortuny.com

Vintage rugs: www.ashleydarryl.com

Carpet: www.starkcarpet.com

"Captain's Chair": www.asherisraelo.com

Oil and collage on canvas artwork: www.frasertaylor.com

End table: www.andriannashamarisinc.com

Desk and side chair: www.maisongerard.com

Chandelier and table lamp: www.arteriorshome.com

Floor lamp: www.circalighting.com

# SOURCES

Contractor:
John Cappa Homes and Construction

Valence and curtain labor:
Marks and Tavano Workroom

### ACADEMY MANSION
### THE GUEST BEDROOM

#### PAGES 108–111
#### PLUMRIDGEHOUSE I SUZANNE EASON
#### 2011—DARK & STORMY: A CAUTIONARY TALE OF HALLOWEEN

Thomas Pheasant wing chairs: www.bakerfurniture.com

Paint: www.benjaminmoore.com

Oil painting over mural: www.kathybuist.com

Black and white photography series: www.chipforelli.com

Chandelier, crystal stemware, china, barware, and silverware: www.hermes.com

Custom ottoman: www.suzanneeason.com

Claw tongs, frames, and feather sculpture: www.michaelaram.com

Branch drinks table: www.mgbwhome.com

Artwork: www.nyaa.edu

Mink throw and pillows: www.pologeorgis.com

Lamps: www.portaromana.com

Dessert plates: www.roberthaviland-cparlon.fr

Fabric on pillows and drapery: www.robertallendesign.com

Carpet: www.starkcarpet.com

Empire sideboard: www.thomaspheasant.com

Wall covering on ceiling: www.troveline.com

#### PAGES 112–113
#### J. COHLER MASON DESIGN
#### 2013—NEW YEAR'S DAY

Wall covering: www.phillipjeffries.com

Ceiling wall covering: www.mayaromanoff.com

Trim paint: www.benjaminmoore.com

Chandelier and mirror above desk: www.johnsalibello.com

Area rug, chair seat fabric, pillows on chairs, pillows on sofa, throw on sofa, and chair seat fabric: www.hollandandsherry.com

Drapery, trim on drapery, and sofa fabric: www.christopherhyland.com

Trim on valence, trim on bench, and trim on sofa: www.samuelandsons.com

Mirrored mantel: S.M. Saber

Art over mantel: www.jimkempnerfineart.com

Deborah Kass pictures: www.deborahkass.com

Pair of chairs: www.venfieldnyc.com

Bench: www.leecalicchioltd.com

Hide on bench: www.edelmanleather.com

Coffee table, desk, and desk chair: www.lorinmarsh.com

Gray object beside books on bottom shelf of bookcase, wine bucket on coffee table, quartz cluster, and box on desk: www.barneys.com

Books: www.assouline.com

Plant in window: www.lexingtongardensnyc.com

Sofa: www.thenewtraditionalists.com

Photograph behind sofa: www.bonnibenrubigallery.com

Sofa side tables: www.donghia.com

Blue champagne flutes: www.baccarat.com

Sculpture on pedestal: www.flairhomecollection.com

#### PAGES 114–115
#### PATRICK JAMES HAMILTON DESIGNS
#### 2014—DERBY DECONSTRUCTED

Artwork: www.aaronsmithart.com; www.babetteherschberger.com; www.clampart.com; www.danromerart.com; www.20thcenturybyhkfa.com

Pharmacy lamp: www.arudin.com

Oval chairs: www.curreycodealers.com

Light fixture: www.abyulighting.com

Gilding: www.alphaworkshops.org

Coffee table book: www.assouline.com

*Tête-à-tête*: www.averyboardman.com

Porcelain vases: www.bealestudio.com

Brass chest: www.barnhardt.biz

Horse statue: www.bungalow5.com

Carpet: www.josephcarinicarpets.com

Gold and glass side table: www.donghia.com

Drapery tiebacks: www.sahco.com

Table lamp: www.1stdibs.com/dealers/highland-park

Gold side table: www.hollyhunt.com

All textiles: www.jab.de

Fire screen: www.johnlyledesign.com

Drapery workroom: www.marksandtavano.com

White side table: www.mgbwhome.com

Flowers: www.ndi.com

Wall covering and ceiling: www.thibautdesign.com

Upholstered wall: www.theworkroomny.com

Embroidery: www.villasavoia.us

Coffee table and desk: www.wisteria.com

#### PAGES 116–117
#### BRETT DESIGN INC.
#### 2012—VALENTINE'S DAY

Small lense table: www.hollyhunt.com

Light fixture: www.baroncelli.com

Carpet (Brett Design for DLB): www.dorisleslieblau.com

Construction: Nick Crumm

Brett Design chaises and bookcases: www.profilesny.net

Photography by Olivier Barbieri: Yancy Richardson Gallery

#### PAGES 118–119
#### DARRIN VARDEN DESIGN
#### 2013—WINTER SOLSTICE

Coffee table fabrication, sofa side tables, bar unit by Darrin Varden, and knife-pleated panels for perimeter of room: www.ivywoodworking.com

Zach armchairs and Laxamana sofa: www.brightchair.com

Ebonized and silver ceruse finish for the custom Darrin Varden-designed coffee table: www.christophepourny.com

Slab of black absolute granite for the coffee table top: www.artistictile.com

Round, custom, dark-navy hand-tufted lux nylon rug: www.crosbystreetstudios.com

Fabric for the trio of pillows on the Darrin Varden Design-custom ottoman: www.casamance.com

Painting and priming: www.paint-tech.com

Art installation: www.ilevel.biz

Chandelier: www.rollandhill.com

Lucite lounge chair: www.designlush.com

Window treatments: www.mtcustom.com

Wall-to-wall carpeting: www.karastan.com

Moving services: www.englebertsmoving.com

Paint: www.benjaminmoore.com

Barware: www.lenox.com

Floral arrangements: www.fleurdepascal.com

Leather on Zach armchairs: www.mooreandgiles.com

Tuul wool sateen for Laxamana sofa: www.brochier.it

"Benthos 2" from the Tehom Series: www.angelomusco.com

Coffee table and side-table accessories: www.johnsalibello.com

Custom-designed ottoman fabric: www.pollackassociates.com

Fabrication and upholstery of custom ottoman and Lucite chair cushion upholstery: www.naulaworkshop.com

# SOURCES

Lucite chair cushion fabric, Laxamana sofa-back cushion, and lumbar pillow fabric: www.brunotriplet.com

**PAGES 120–121**
**WEITZMAN HALPERN INTERIOR DESIGN**
**2013—SWEET SIXTEEN**

Wall covering: www.astekwallcovering.com

Furniture: www.averyboardman.com; www.cb2.com; www.knoll.com; Niedermaier; www.venfieldnyc.com

Carpet and rugs: www.crosbystreetstudios.com; www.starkcarpet.com; www.houseoftaiping.com

Accessories: www.currenthomeny.com; www.jonathanadler.com; www.johnsalibello.com; www.maison24.com

Floor lamp: www.dwr.com

Wallpaper: www.flavorpaper.com

Valence fabric and shades: www.glant.com; www.romo.com

Upholstery: www.jpcustomupholstery.co

Lamp on desk: www.jcpenney.com

Window treatments: www.mergencestudios.com

Mirrors: www.kartell.com

**PAGES 122–123**
**DREW McGUKIN INTERIORS**
**SPONSORED BY ROBERT ALLEN**
**2015—SUMMER SOLSTICE**

All fabrics, paperbacked walls and ceiling, metal frame armchair, and upholstered ottoman: www.robertallendesign.com

Decorative table lamps at sofa: www.visualcomfortlightinglights.com

Table lamp at chest, floor lamp, and accessories: www.arteriorshome.com

Drapery hardware: www.4thstatemetals.com

Trim paint: www.farrow-ball.com

Small set of paintings near sofa: www.kellyneidig.com

DMC custom designed, painted mirror with steel shelf: www.timothypoe.com

Sofa and lounge chair: Swaim

Draperies: Marcia Levine Workroom

Painting of Hampton's beachscape: Kristin's Beach Home

All wall coverings: JD Paperhanging Corp.

**PAGES 124–125**
**DÉCOR BY GUILLAUME GENTET, INC.**
**2014—HONEYMOON IN PARIS**

Drapery fabric, headboard, and footboard fabric, desk chair fabric, and trim: www.robertallendesign.com

"Breakfast in St. Tropez" artwork: www.chesleymclaren.com

Paint: www.farrow-ball.com

White window sculpture by Thomas Malley: www.fieldgallery.com

Antique restoration: www.jimgreeneboxes.com

Bedside wall lamps: www.lampworks.com

Fabrication: www.leonardosupholstery.com

Headboard, footboard, and desk chair: www.louisjsolomon

Chandelier: www.tisserant.fr

Serving pieces and lamp: www.michaelaram.com

Carpeting and border: www.starkcarpet.com

Mattress and box spring: www.sleepstudio.com

Artwork above headboard: www.gitanarosa.com/Nathaniel-galka/

Wallcovering design, antique *secretaire à abattant*, and artwork: Guillaume Gentet

Base coating and wallpaper installation: Imperative Painting, Brooklyn, NY: (718) 743-6545

## ACADEMY MANSION THE TOP FLOOR BALLROOM

**PAGES 128–129**
**HUNTLEY & CO. INTERIOR DESIGN**
**2012—A HOLIDAY LUNCHEON HOSTED BY A MODERN-DAY MARIE ANTOINETTE**

Furniture: www.roche-bobois.com

Light fixtures: www.lladro.com

Textiles: www.huttoncollections.com

Fabric: www.pierrefrey.com

Mirror/TV: www.audiodoctor.com

**PAGES 130–131**
**ALLY COULTER DESIGNS**
**2013—'TIS THE SEASON**

Woodwork: www.woodmeister.com

Window treatments: www.manhattanshade.com; www.yourhomestore.com

Fabric: www.christopherhyland.com

Furniture: www.dedar.com; www.roche-bobois.com; www.dakotajackson.com; www.martinalbert.com

Furniture and accessories: www.ralphlauren.com

Crystal accessories: www.baccarat.com

Accessories: www.tiffany.com

Bar stools and accessories: www.johnlyledesign.com

Rug: www.kylebunting.com

Wall covering: www.mayaromanoff.com

Frames: www.jpocker.com

Sound system: www.savant.com

Decorative painting: www.metamorfaux-decorative-painting.com

**PAGES 132–133**
**JUSTIN SHAULIS, INC.**
**2014—GALLERY HOPPING IN MIAMI**

Custom area rug: www.crosbystreetstudios.com

Upholstery, coffee tables, and end tables: www.lazzoni.us

Hand-painted acrylic coffee table: www.sublime-living.com

Drapery construction: www.xperienceworkroom.com

Accessories: www.justinshaulis.com

Custom bar and coffee table: www.pryorcallaway.com

Artwork: www.shennavaughn.com; www.islandweiss.com; www.dorfmanplus.com; www.berrycampbell.com; www.hellergallery.com; www.upriseart.com

Art advisor: www.esadoff.com

Lighting design: www.urbansteeldesign.com

Table lamps: www.blackbody.fr

Fine art shipping and delivery: lucie.poisson@yahoo.com

Production Assistants: Elizabeth Bates, Jordan Kronquist, and Scott Lilly

**PAGES 134–135**
**VICENTE WOLF ASSOCIATES, INC.**
**2015—GLAMPING**

Astro-turf: www.foxfloors.com

Geodesic pod: www.pacificdomes.com

Bed, rug, bed linens, towels, and accessories: www.calvinklein.com

Mural: www.muralsyourway.com

Wall graphic: www.eeny.net

Audio and video: www.vicentewolf.com

Bathtub: www.dxv.com

Trees: www.americanfoliagedesign.com

## WATERMILL 2016

**PAGES 140–141**
**MADDUX CREATIVE**
**2016—CORNWALL COASTLINE**

Reclaimed barn-wood table and plinth "Louise": www.barninthecity.com

Vine 8 chandelier: www.mattermatters.com

Rug: www.vanderhurd.com; www.therugcompany.com

Huang chair, plinth, scroll screen, set of 2 root tables, and chalice side table: www.robertkuo.com

Light up table sculpture, Stefan sculpture, Cataline sculpture, Aris concave pedestal, large Aris concave pedestal, vintage brass sail sculpture, and vintage Maitland-Smith travertine sculpture: www.flairhomecollection.com

Chandelier and sconces: www.ochre.net

Accessories: www.newel.com; www.bkantiques.com

Paint: www.farrow-ball.com

Plants: www.broadviewgardenseh.com

Painter: Isabelle Day

# SOURCES

**PAGES 142–143**
**HB HOME**
**2016—PARTY IN PANTELLERIA**

Table: www.dessinfournir.com

Custom mobile: www.modmobiles.com

Sectional: www.huttoncollections.com

Fabric on ottoman: www.pavoni.com

Fabric on daybed: www.dedar.com

Fabric on chairs: www.clarencehouse.com

Drapery fabric: www.hbluxe.com

**PAGES 144–147**
**MABLEY HANDLER INTERIOR DESIGN**
**2016—GRADUATION DAY**

Accessories: www.michellehatchny.com

Wallpaper: www.phillipjeffries.com

Light fixtures: www.ro-sham-beaux.com

Rug: www.therugcompany.com

Windows: www.theshadestore.com

Carpet: www.starkcarpet.com

Furniture: www.worlds-away.com; www.oomphonline.com; www.mecox.com

**PAGES 148–149**
**CHAD JAMES GROUP**
**2016—MAY DAY**

Center table, silver photographs, stool, mirror, bench, three tables, and mirrored-top end tables: www.newel.com

Rug: www.therugcompany.com

Sofa: www.dmitriyco.com

Steel boxes, bookends, nickel stands, crystals, and agate pillow: www.kimberlymcdonald.com

Side table, heart chair, and lounge chair: www.jerrypair.com

Caleido, folio, and linen print: www.scalamandre.com

High-wire tandem: www.apparatusstudio.com

Prima alpaca: www.sandrajordan.com

Floor lamp: www.hollandandsherry.com

"Future Site of Expensive Painting" artwork: www.dorfmanplus.com

**PAGES 150–151**
**BALTIMORE DESIGN GROUP**
**2016—HARVEST EAST END**

Installation of wallpaper and mural: www.allislandpainting.com

Floral wallpaper and floral mural: www.flavorpaper.com

Accessories and furniture: www.baltimoredesigncenter.com

**PAGES 152–153**
**2 MICHAELS DESIGN**
**2016—INTERNATIONAL WOMEN'S DAY**

Curtain fabric: www.jab.de

Draperies: www.contractworkroom.com

Rug: www.saccocarpet.com

Contractor: www.wisesolutionshamptons.com

Desk: www.magenxxcentury.com

Photo by Sam Samore: www.teamgal.com

Desk chair: www.1stdibs.com

Desk lamp: www.lunamodern.com

Conference table: www.weinbergmodern.com

Conference chairs: www.magenxxcentury.com

Wall sculpture: www.suzannetick.com

Eye sconce: www.1stdibs.com

Settee: www.toddmerrillstudio.com

Coffee table: www.magenxxcentury.com

Crescent chairs and wall sculpture by Chesney's: www.1stdibs.com

Side table: www.weinbergmodern.com

Bust sculptures: www.allanstoneprojects.com

Black and white photos: www.robinricegallery.com

Console: www.bgoecklerantiques.com

**PAGES 154–155**
**TIMOTHY BROWN STUDIO**
**2016—FATHER'S DAY**

Ping-Pong table: www.blattbilliards.com

Painter: www.dbpaintinganddecoratinginc.com

Furniture: www.dedon.de; www.dualoy.com; www.flessasdesign.com; www.hollyhunt.com; www.interiorsbyeandj.com

Antiques: www.jackandmarcel.com; R.E. Steels Antiques

Artwork: www.laurenhwangnewyork.com

Textiles: www.rogersandgoffigon.com

Carpet: www.saccocarpet.com

Accessories: www.timothybrownstudio.com

**PAGES 156–157**
**JOLIE KOREK & CO.**
**2016—SUMMER SOLSTICE**

Design coordinator: Lisa Meskin

Sofa, fabric on sofa, cocktail table, side table, drink table, bedside tables, and wallpaper: www.hollyhunt.com

Lucite and driftwood stool: www.timothyoulton.com

Stone tops: www.majestickitchens.com

Nymph lamps: www.donghia.com

Artwork curated by: www.ericfirestonegallery.com

Chandelier: www.ochre.net

Master bed: Jolie Korek & Co. and Hot Pass Fabrication

Bed and headboard fabric: www.castelmaisoncom

Bedding: www.abchome.com

Upholstery and window treatments: Fallou Workroom

Wall panels: Jolie Korek & Co. and Fabricio Fabri

Wall treatment: Fabricio Fabri

Wall panels and carpentry: www.mjccarpentry.com

Window fabric: www.hollyhunt.com

Audio installation: www.hiframe.com

Rug: www.odegardcarpets.com

Wine station: www.dacor.com

**PAGES 158–159**
**WESLEY MOON, INC.**
**2016—PALM SUNDAY**

Bed and mattress: www.savoirbeds.com

Nightstands, pair of benches, and mirror: www.johnsalibello.com

Sofa: Refine Modern

Coffee table and chest of drawers: www.tuckerrobbins.com

Lounge chair: www.mydesignermichael.com

End tables: www.valeriegoodmangallery.com

Vanity table, vanity chair, and floor lamp: www.vandenakkerantiques.com

Bathroom bench: www.fivefingerfurnishings.com

Bedroom chandelier: www.gaspareasaro.com

Bedside lamps: www.kimilletaylor.com

Swing-arm lamps: www.circalighting.com

Chest lamp: www.studiovandenakker.com

Hallway sconces: www.gaspareasaro.com

Hallway ceiling fixture: www.delapuenteantiques.com

Main area rug: www.fjhakimian.com

Hallway runner: www.starkcarpet.com

Bathroom area rug: www.therugstore.com

Artwork by window ("Mondello Paddle Boats" by Massimo Vitali) and artwork on hallway closet doors ("The Bikini Girl on the Boardwalk" & "Catherine and Her Surfboard" by Georges Dambier): www.benrubigallery.com

Artwork over sofa ("Printemps" by Peter Hoffer): www.markelfinearts.com

Bathroom stools and artwork beside bed ("Set of 20 Gold Ceramic Bubbles" by Stacy Cushman): www.cocobolodesign.com

Artwork on hallway side wall (set of 4 Von Allen paintings): www.quoguegallery.com

Small artwork ("Baby Pieces," Mixed Media by Darlene Charneco), artwork over vanity ("The Secret Garden" by Maria Berrio), and artwork in bathroom ("Small Works" by Sofia Quino): www.praxis-art.com/en

# SOURCES

**PAGES 160–163**
**MELANIE ROY DESIGN**
**2016—EARTH DAY**

Round mirror: www.arteriorshome.com

Tim Bessell surfboard and Francine Tint painting over desk: www.chaseedwardsgallery.com

Bedside tables: www.ercolehome.com

Photograph: www.igifineart.com

Crystal lamps: www.kravet.com

Desk: www.lorinmarsh.com

Trays: www.madegoods.com

Accessories: www.mecox.com

Vladimir Kagan chaise: Refine Modern

Interior crafts and chandelier: Emanuel Morez

Pebble table: www.phillipscollection.org

Wallpaper, fur throw, pillows, and curtain fabric: www.romo.com

Shag rug: www.starkcarpet.com

Outdoor rug: www.therugcompany.com

Milo Baughman bed: Scarborough Antique

Benches: www.toddmerrillstudio.com

Standing lamp: www.vaughandesigns.com

Outdoor furniture and swing: www.dedon.de

Outdoor cement tables: www.osoindustries.com

**PAGES 164–165**
**BARBARA OSTROM & ASSOCIATES**
**2016—STAYCATION DAY**

Graffiti wall covering: www.pierrefrey.com

Black wall covering: www.phillipjeffries.com

Rug: www.therugcompany.com

Mural: www.andrewtedesco.com

Renderer: Boris Reyt

TV/fireplace: In Tech-Hi Frame Screen Design

Workbench: NJC Contracting Corporation

Painters: www.badillapainters.com

Gym equipment: www.gymsource.com

Hanging surfboards: www.flyingpointsurf.com

Oil painting: www.kevinmcferrin.com

Accessories: www.englishcountryantiques.blogspot.com

Refrigerator: www.smegusa.com

Game chairs: www.artisticframe.com

Paint: www.farrow-ball.com

Sofa: www.biasicatani.com

Bicycles: www.martonecycling.com

Light fixtures: www.suffolkdesignerlighting.com

Car: www.porsche.com

Orange seatbelt chairs, bicycle chairs, and round table next to sofa: www.phillipscollection.org

Wooden man chair: www.tuckerrobbins.com

Throw pillows, clock, and accessories: www.hildreths.com

Mural artist for tire graffiti on floor: Andrew Tedesco

## BRIDGEHAMPTON 2013

**PAGES 168–169**
**DONNA LIVINGSTON DESIGN**
**2013—RENEWAL DAY & THE CELEBRATION OF WOMEN**

"Yonder" painting: www.frankbowling.com

"Natural Beauty" photograph: www.farber.com

"Standing Woman" sculpture: www.roberthookesculpture.com

"Madonna" sculpture: www.jdhansen.com

"Mesh Woman" sculpture: www.davidbegbie.com

Elfenbein chair: www.maxidny.com

Chandelier and bench: www.englishcountryantiques.blogspot.com

Console: www.formationsusa.com

Center table: www.gregoriuspineo.com

Pillows: www.missoni.com

Staircase rug: www.starkcarpet.com

Area rug: www.amadicarpets.com

Drapery: www.donghia.com

"The Fountain of Youth" floral design: Brent Wang

**PAGES 170–173**
**THOM FILICIA, INC.**
**2013—HHH**

Curtain hardware, rug, throw blanket, pillows, bookcases, custom hanging fixture, floor lamps, vintage concentric sculpture, artisanal books, paintings by Vincent Brandi, wall sconce, and wood veneer wall covering: www.sedgwickandbrattle.com

Sectional sofa, chairs, ottoman, floor mirror, and all fabrics: www.kravet.com

Bamboo table, antique jars, shagreen boxes, feliciano bejar magiscope, and centerpiece bowl: www.1stdibs.com

Lucite pedestals: www.bakerfurniture.com

Ebonized console: www.craigvandenbrulle.com

Lyell pedestals: www.donghia.com

Rug: www.saccocarpet.com

End table, armchair, eagle sculpture, horse hitch, and woven cream fiber: www.wyeth.nyc

Vase, trays, votives, square dish, and rectangular dish: www.bernardaud.com

Deconstructed lobster, clawed lobster, ammonite pair, narwhal tusk, claire palastanga, and ceramic urchins: www.creelandgow.com

Art pieces by Suzi Matthews, teak, and stainless lantern: www.store.comerfordcollection.com

Malmaison decanter, round tray, small and medium bowl, ice bucket, server set, large cluny vase, vertigo menu holder, vertigo tray, malmaison underplate, and perle frames: www.christofle.com

Munich table lamp: www.dennismiller.com

Artwork by Scott Redden, volcano basket, sitting man sculpture, and assorted books: www.mecox.com

Art and design books: www.pointedleafpress.com; www.crownpublishing.com

Bar hardware: www.hamiltonsinkler.com

Salt and pepper shakers, antique tray, blue glass vases, wine bucket, stool, horn, and BB English bucket: www.englishcountryantiques.blogspot.com

Iron wall sculpture, garden stool, and table set: www.johnsalibello.com

Wine: www.wölffer.com

Switchplates and dimmers: www.legrand.us

"Electronic Circuitry Box" by Theo Kamecke: www.lorinmarsh.com

Curtain fabrication and installation: www.calicocorners.com

Moving and storage: www.celebritymoving.com

Contractor services: www.fanuka.com

**PAGES 174–175**
**RICHARD MISHAAN DESIGN**
**2013—YVES KLEIN BLUE DINING ROOM**

Dining table, buffet, chairs and window treatments: www.homerdesign.com

Curtain fabric: www.donghia.com

Roman shade fabric: www.kravet.com

Rug: www.therugcompany.com

Metal sculpture: R.E. Steele Antiques

Pendant lights: www.urbanelectricco.com

Sconces: www.richardmishaan.com

China, glassware, and flatware: www.lenox.com

Napkins and table runner: www.suntexdesigns.com

Ceramic vases: www.bernardaud.com

Crystal vases: www.baccarat.com

Wallpaper: Wall Art, LLC

Paint: www.c2paint.com

Wallpaper installation: New England Wallpapering

**PAGES 176–179**
**MABLEY HANDLER INTERIOR DESIGN**
**2013—IN BY MEMORIAL DAY**

Fabric: www.leejofa.com; www.kravet.com

Furniture: www.mrbrownhome.com; www.homefurniturenyc.com; www.oomphonline.com; www.mecox.com

Accessories: www.michellehatchny.com

Rug: www.customcoolrugs.com

Lighting: www.helenbilt.com

Artwork: Susan Vecsey Artwork

Wallpaper: www.phillipjeffries.com

Fireplace: www.chesneys.com

# SOURCES

Paint: www.c2paint.com

Candles: www.glassbaby.com

**PAGES 180–181**
**MARSHALL WATSON INTERIORS**
**2013—MIDSUMMER NIGHT: THE SWEDISH SUMMER SOLSTICE**

Decorative painting on walls and other painting: Judy Mulligan

Rug: www.dorislesliebIau.com

Bed, sofa, armchair, and left side table (from Marshall Watson collection for Ferrell Mittman): www.ef-lm.com

Mirror and right side table: www.mecox.com

Round and square wood tables, and sofa side tables: www.johnhoushmand.com

Lamp shades, decorative pillows, and throws: www.gracioushome.com

Curtain fabric, bed canopy, and headboard fabric: www.zimmer-rohde.com

Bed linens: www.juliab.com

Silver vases: www.christofle.com

Lamps: www.johnsalibello.com

**PAGES 182–183**
**TAMARA MAGEL**
**2013—BEACH CHIC**

Wallpaper by Tamara Magel: www.starkcarpet.com

Wallpaper on opposite wall: www.phillipjeffries.com

Accessories: www.englishcountryantiques.blogspot.com

**PAGES 184–185**
**DÉCOR BY GUILLAUME GENTET, INC.**
**2013—BASTILLE DAY**

Artwork: ww.chesleymclaren.com

Pillows: www.fischbacher.com; www.creations-metaphores.com

Wood molding, doors, and baseboards: www.dykeslumber.com

In-wall invisible speakers: www.extremeavs.com

Wall sconces and pedestal (finish by Guillaume Gentet): www.globalviews.com

Eiffel Tower model: www.mercigustave.com

Sofas, cocktail table, consoles, and chandelier: www.roche-bobois.com

Trim and tie backs: www.samuelandsons.com

Mirror TV: www.seura.com

Orchids and Topiaries: SilverLeaf

Carpeting: www.starkcarpet.com

Candelabra: www.studioa-home.com

Drapery fabric: Verel de Belval

Macaroons: www.ladurée.com

Pink game table: Guillaume Gentet

Hardware and Marie Antoinette bows: Private collection

**PAGES 186–187**
**INSON DUBOIS WOOD, LLC.**
**2013—FOURTH OF JULY**

Stereo: www.audiodoctor.com

Lighting: www.baroncelli.com

Stone mantel: www.chesneys.com

Window treatments: www.christopherhyland.com

Rug: www.dorisleslieblau.com; www.fjhakimian.com

Ferrari: www.dupontregistry.com

Pillows: www.fortuny.com; www.lesageinterieurs.com

Wallpaper: www.graciestudio.com; www.phillipjeffries.com

Metal side tables: www.johnlyledesign.com

Ceramics: www.lladro.com

Painting: www.michaeldickeyart.com

Wood walls: www.westflooring.com

Organic lacquer chaise: www.insonwood.com

**PAGES 188–189**
**ELIZABETH BOLOGNINO INTERIORS, LLC.**
**2013—AFTERGLOW**

Outdoor furniture: www.dedon.de; www.calazzo.com

Decorative tiles: www.mosaichse.com

Photography: www.bobtaborimages.com

## SAG HARBOR 2014

**PAGES 192–193**
**HUNIFORD DESIGN STUDIO**
**2014—LABOR DAY**

Custom-designed crescent sofa, hanging leather chair with throw pillow, custom wooden side table, area rug, dining table with benches, pair of acrylic globe lamps with shades, leather floor pillows, Brazilian geode sculpture with marble base, books, glass vessel, metal spring, metal tray, pair of rectangular throw pillows, circular throw pillow, carved marble tazza, silvered metal vase, silvered metal bowl by Ward Bennett, glass jar vessel, pottery vase holding utensils, pottery vase, set of three metal chargers, wooden bowl on counter, metal tray, wooden tray, pipe ceiling fixture, set of three cage ceiling fixtures, whale bone sculpture, clipboards by Huniford, ladder, "Pure" sign, set of concrete drums, and wooden pencil sculpture: www.huniford.com

Suar slice coffee table: www.chista.net

Pair of cubist armchairs and set of four stools: www.1stdibs.com

Concrete accessories, wooden bowl, linen sheet towel, and black stoneware vases: www.calvinklein.com

Resin sphere sculpture with encased watch elements: www.solo-modern.com

Pair of sea-grass runners: www.pattersonflynnmartin.com

Artwork: www.pacegallery.com; www.cheimread.com; www.saranightingale.com

Rug: www.fjhakimian.com

Furniture: www.thewarehouse440.com

**PAGES 194–195**
**BJØRNEN DESIGN**
**2014—SEAHORSE COUNTRY**

Upholstery: www.nycustomfurnishings.com

Carpet: www.stephanieodegard.com

Fabric: www.kravet.com; www.leejofa.com

Window treatments and pillows: www.hamptonwindowstyle.com

Photography: www.robinricegallery.com

Custom cabinetry: www.californiaclosets.com

Coffee table: www.mecox.com

Throw and accessories: www.fishershomefurnishings.com

Wall coverings: www.phillipjeffries.com

Wallpapering: Jamie Haeger

Electrician: M&B Electric

Painting: www.edslandscaping.com

Floral arrangement: www.sagharborflorist.net

Ceiling light: www.chandelierfinelighting.com

Audio and visual: System Designs

Bronze nautilus: www.jedjohnson.com

Bath terrarium: Joseph Cornetta Design

**PAGES 196–197**
**ID CREATIONS**
**2014—BUNGALOW**

Rug: www.fjhakimian.com

Accessories: www.vicentewolf.com

Console: www.ercole.com

Artwork: www.dorfmanprojects.com

End table: www.lorinmarsh.com

Light fixture: www.interieurs.com

Sofa: www.ef-lm.com

Coffee table: www.nancycorzine.com

Pillows: www.biasicatani.com

## SOHO 2016

**PAGES 202–203**
**JAIME WALTERS**
**2016—LOCAL MAKERS FRIENDSGIVING**

Wallpaper: Calico; info@calicowallpaper.com

Tabletop and holiday décor: www.gilt.com

Lounge chair and stool: Erickson Aesthetics; info@ericksonaesthetics.com

Table, counter stool, and dining chair: Uhuru; info@uhurudesign.com

Dry bar: Token; info@tokennyc.com

Farrago pendant: Roll and Hill; info@rollandhill.com

Cinema: Rich Brilliant Willing

Rug: Aelfie; hello@aelfie.com

Portraits: Mae Elvis; maeelvis@gmail.com

# SOURCES

"I Woke Up in a Dream" Print: Andrew De Francesco; Andrew.defrancesco@gmail.com

Pottery and sculpture: Nicholas Newcomb; info@nicholasnewcomb.com

**PAGES 204–205**
**SASHA BIKOFF INTERIOR DESIGN**
**2016—ROSÉ ALL DAY**

Dining table, champagne bucket, and bronze centerpiece: www.newel.com

Wallpaper: www.pierrefrey.com

Chandelier: www.cosulichinteriors.com

Drapes: www.christopherhyland.com

Drapery hardware and installation: www.theshadestore.com

Zig-zag chairs, lacquer and brass sideboard, fan mirror, and pair of lamps: www.sashabikoff.com

Peacock: www.creelandgow.com

All tabletops: www.scullyandscully.com

**PAGES 206–207**
**MEREDITH OSTROM**
**2016—HAPPY BIRD DAY**

Wallpaper mural on walls and drapery fabric: www.osbourneandlittle.com

Bird wallpaper mural on ceiling: www.hollyhunt.com

Wallpaper hanging and painting: www.badillapainters.com

Drapery workroom: Baum Draperies

Lighting: www.lladro.com

Headshot: www.antoineverglas.com

Furniture: www.poltronafrau.com; www.cassina.com; www.cappellini.com

TV strip unit: Intech-High Frame

Frying-pan mirror and sex cake sculpture: www.carpentersworkshopgallery.com

Video art: www.seditionart.com

Paint: www.farrow-ball.com

Plates, wine glasses, and napkins: www.scullyandscully.com

Plates: www.christopherspitzmiller.com

Artwork: www.studiojob.be

Video: Marco Brambilla

Painting on back wall: Meredith Ostrom

**PAGES 208–209**
**CAMPION PLATT INTERIORS**
**2016—BLACK FRIDAY**

Fabrics for walls, upholstery, windows, Pangaea in malachite, rutilus in anthracite, fur in silica, octopus fleece in black, iguana in gold mustard, Vaalbara in anthracite, sea sand and gold, and Gondwana in anthracite: www.alcantara.com

Furniture, accessories, Roman wing chair, dining table, side chair, chandelier, floor lamp, bar cart, table lamp, buffet, fur ottoman, and wood mirror: Mitchell Gold and Bob Williams

Rug: www.fjhakimian.com

All artwork: www.cure8group.com

Glass artist, candleholders, and hand-blown glass: www.moshebursuker.com

Contractor: www.interiormanagement.com

**PAGES 210–211**
**BRADFIELD & TOBIN**
**2016—ARTISTIC LICENSE**

Draperies, sofa, pillows, pillow fabric, and wall covering: www.jab.de

Carpet: www.starkcarpet.com

Chairs, consoles, torchières, side tables, and chandeliers: www.johnsalibello.com

Custom sofa and upholstery: www.fineartsfurn.com

Drapery: www.interiorsbyroyale.com

Custom fireplace: www.besagawoodworking.com

Painting services: Dalcro Interiors

Parrot sculptures: www.sculpturesworld.com

Hugo Bastidas paintings: www.nohrahaimegallery.com

Iceberg sculpture: www.leilahellergallery.com

Paint: www.farrow-ball.com

**PAGES 212–213**
**HARRY HEISSMANN, INC.**
**2016—B/W CHRISTMAS**

Carousel zebra: www.yewtreehouseantiques.com

Wallpaper: www.starkwallcovering.com

Wallpaper installation: AU Wallcovering Inc.

Paint: www.farrow-ball.com

Carpet: www.starkcarpet.com

Bed: www.lobelmodern.com

Linens, towels, and bathroom accessories: www.ebraunnewyork.com

Screen fabric: www.pierrefrey.com

Screen fabrication: www.victoriaandson.com; www.manhattanshade.com

"Cloud" tables: www.valeriegoodmangallery.com

Pair of lamps: www.christopherspitzmiller.com

Pair of baluster elements: www.victoriaandson.com

Wall mirror, tulip chair, full-moon light sculpture, and hand-blown soda glass: www.r-and-company.com

Game table and taboret: www.lizobrien.com

Contracting services and project management: www.elementdesignnyc.com

Moving, transporting, and logistics: www.windsorcompany.com

Room illustration: www.philliporozco.com

Decorative pillow and pillow fabrication: www.startcarpet.com

Pom-pom trim and pom-pom fringe color: www.samuelandsons.com

Pillow fabrication: Maureen McNamee

**PAGES 214–215**
**CAPITAL C INTERIORS**
**2016—WORLD ART DAY**

Fauteuil: www.acroterion.1stdibs.com

Isabella Clara Eugenia mixed media: www.alexiszambrano.com

Drapery and upholstery installation: www.anthonylawrence.com

Headboard and bed frame: www.averyboardman.com

Custom lampshade: www.blanchefield.com

Mattress: www.coco-mat.com

Bed linens: www.deborahsharpelinens.com

Bed basics: www.downrightltd.com

Specialty art lighting: www.erco.com

Paint and wallpaper: www.farrow-ball.com

Flowers: www.flowersbyspecialarrangement.com

Art transportation and installation for Ran Ortner: www.ganderandwhite.com

Armchair and side table: www.jeandemerry.com

Bedroom chandelier: www.lindseyadelman.com

Bedside table and bed bench: www.lizobrien.com

Scented candles, perfume diffuser, and porcelain swim figurine: www.lladro.com

Decorative and fine paint: www.markchamberlainpainting.com

Wallpaper installation, wall décor, and wallpaper hanging: Michael Lanza

Closet stylist: www.morphewconcept.com

Improvisation wood: www.peterhoffmanart.com

"Element No. 34" oil on canvas: www.ranortner.com

Armchair and closet valet: www.roche-bobois.com

All upholstery, drapery fabrics, and trim: www.robertallendesign.com

"Hotpoint" oil on linen: www.robertszot.com

Wallpaper in bedroom: www.donghia.com

Carpet: www.starkcarpet.com

Wall side mirrors: www.suiteny.com

Window blinds: www.theshadestore.com

Vanity table: www.vandenakkerantiques.com

Plug-in lamps and bathroom ceiling pendant: www.vaughandesigns.com

Table: www.johnlyledesign.com

**PAGES 216–217**
**PATRICK MCGRATH DESIGN**
**2016—HIS DRESSING ROOM**

Gray painted canapé, spinario sculpture, and marble Roman bust: www.christies.com

Six John Currin etchings: www.gagosian.com

Thai silk flat-weave rug: www.fortstreetstudio.com

# SOURCES

Armchair with sabots, nesting tables, lantern, and paginated bronze: www.maisongerard.com

Vintage fluted and ebonized column: www.michaelbargo.com

Vance New York painting: www.1stdibs.com

Desk, commode, and wooden mirror: www.patrickmcgrathdesign.com

Wall sculpture: www.paulmorehouse.com

Curtain panels: www.loropiana.com

Paint: www.farrow-ball.com

Workrooms: www.rosenfeldinteriors.com; www.mhgstudio.com

**PAGES 218–219**
**CHARLES J. NAFIE ARCHITECTS**
**2016—BEDAZZLED CANOPY**

Lighting: www.mskilluminations.com

Powder room: www.clsterling.com

Powder room lighting: www.lladro.com

Paint: www.farrow-ball.com

Wall covering: www.brettdesigninc.com

Rugs: www.dorisleslieblau.com

Furniture: www.maisongerard.com

Bench: www.bgoecklerantiques.com

Painting contractor: Caltech Construction

Electrical contractor: E2E Integratech Inc.

Art advisory: www.elizabethfiore.com

**PAGES 220–223**
**TINA RAMCHANDANI CREATIVE**
**2016—THE HAPPIEST HOUR**

All furniture: www.designlush.com

Paint: www.us.farrow-ball.com

Decorative painter: Dennis Alexander Cruz

Window treatments: www.homeinteriorsbyanthony.com

Window treatment fabric: www.stylelibrary.com

Hardware: www.baldwinhardware.com

Rug: www.tufenkiancarpets.com

Art broker: www.artnet.com

Artwork: www.robertwhitman.com

Accessories: www.mattermatters.com; www.hawkinsnewyork.com

Plants: www.flonyevents.com

Towels in bathroom: www.christylinens.com

**PAGES 224–225**
**RC STUDIO**
**2016—AFTER THE BALL DROPS**

Table: www.etageprojects.com

Daybed: www.roomonline.com

Daybed fabric and drapery fabric: www.hollyhunt.com

Wall shelf: www.jonathannesci.com

Mirror: www.palosamko.com

Chair: www.espasso.com

Ceramic stump: www.kierankinsella.com

Aim pendants, table lamp, and floor lamp: www.flos.com

Window treatment, fabrication, and installation: www.manhattanshade.com

Painting, electrical, and hanging: www.argoconstructionny.com

Rug: Direct Line Carpet

Fox throw: www.reichfurs.com

Photo print: David Kukin

Canister: www.monc13.com

**PAGES 226–227**
**RYAN KORBAN**
**2016—LUXURY REDEFINED**

Furniture: www.flairhomecollection.com

Lighting: www.venfieldnyc.com

Mannequins: www.frankgloverproductions.com

Painting: www.jmwconstructioninc.com

Drapery work: www.zarinfabrics.com

Drapery, area rug, and fabrics: www.starkcarpet.com

NuSilk TM carpet: www.stgcarpets.com

Florist: www.barbarascott.com

Mirrors: www.louisjsolomon.com

Paint: www.farrow-ball.com

Coffee table: www.phoenix-gallery.com

**PAGES 228–229**
**JOYCE D. SILVERMAN INTERIORS**
**2016—MAD HATTER ROOFTOP**

Fillo table, fillo mirror, quail, toad, fabric for pillows, wall covering for bathroom, and bath towels set: www.angelabrownltd.com

Painting the pergola and installing bathroom wallpaper: A & L Construction of NY

Pillow upholstery: www.bettertex.com

Rest chair and lounge chair: www.dedon.de

Paint color: www.farrow-ball.com

Area rug: www.pattersonflynnmartin.com

Cupcakes: www.pieceofcakeinc.com

Construction of pergola and lattice: www.sollecitocustomhomes.com

Flooring materials and floor installation: U.C. Workroom Inc.

Dining table, dining chairs, sofa, lounge chairs, and side table: www.walterswicker.com

All floral arrangements: www.louiskonstantinos.com

Donation of ferns: www.associatedcutflower.com

Teacups, saucers, pot, bowl, and tray: www.stillfried.com

Bathroom accessories: www.waterworks.com

## BACK MATTER

**PAGES 241**
**BARBARA OSTROM & ASSOCIATES**
**2010—CHINESE NEW YEAR**

Draperies: www.thibautdesign.com

All tableware: www.scullyandscully.com

Dragon painting on ceiling: www.andrewtedesco.com

Fabric: www.beaconhilldesign.com

Area rug: www.orleyshabahang.com

Flowers: www.flowersoncolumbus.com

Chinese screen: www.bgoecklerantiques.com

Drapery workroom: Baum Draperies

Accessories: www.graciestudio.com

Dining chairs and accessories: Hampton Briggs Antiques at www.1stdibs.com

Accessories and chairs: www.agostinoltd.com

Console: www.davidduncanantiques.com

Vases: www.chineseporcelaincompany.com

Mirror: www.niermannweeks.com

**PAGE 247**
**UNLIMITED EARTH CARE, INC.**
**2016—SPRING EQUINOX**

Producer of planters: www.potterypots.nl

Designer of planters: www.unlimitedearthcare.com

**OPPOSITE PAGE 252**
**RIO HAMILTON**
**SPONSORED BY ROBERT ALLEN**
**2015—GENTLEMEN'S LOUNGE**

Fabric on walls and benches: www.robertallendesign.com

Labor for upholstering walls and making benches: www.naulaworkshop.com

Artist for large framed painting: www.lumarouge.com

18th century French Régence-style frame: www.lowy1907.com

Light pendant: www.curreycodealers.com

Small gold table: www.tuckerrobbins.com

# ACKNOWLEDGMENTS

Iris Dankner, Iris Apfel

Jay, Danielle, Niki, and Iris Dankner

Roric Tobin, Thom Filicia, Iris Dankner, Geoffrey Bradfield

Iris Dankner, Mario Buatta

To my Mom and Dad, thank you for always encouraging me to follow my dreams and allowing me to travel my creative path. Mom, you are the best role model, and I give you full credit for nurturing my sense of style (black with a touch of leopard). Daddy, you've taught me to never give up, to live life to the fullest, and to always remember, 'The best is yet to come.' You are my rock!

To the best sister in the world, Laurel, you are the glue that keeps me together through all phases of life, whether raising our kids, dealing with our parents and husbands, or growing our careers. Thank you for sharing so many amazing adventures, lots of laughs, and countless treasure hunts. I love you, Sis!

To my brother Billy—You still make me feel like a teenager. Our time together is always such fun, but never long enough. I love you, Billy!

To my husband Jay, thank you for always supporting and standing beside me, and being my biggest cheerleader. Most of all, thanks for always putting up with my shenanigans. Fatch, I love you!

My daughters, Niki and Danielle—always follow your passions and remember, no "idea" is too little or too big. I love you from here to the moon and stars and back.

Sam, your advice and business strategy have been priceless. Having you join our family has been a dream come true. I hit the jackpot when it comes to a son-in-law!

To Judith Brisman, thank you for advising me to be the best "me" possible. I could not have done this and so much more without you.

Lancelot Bacchus, the man who has kept me in the best physical (and therefore mental) shape for the past twenty years, thank you for keeping me young and looking my best.

Thank you to all my friends and my BFF's who have been my anchors through it all. My real friends know me and still love me. Thanks for always sticking by me on this crazy ride.

To the industry, creating Holiday House was not an easy task or, as they say, it takes a village. When I first thought of creating Holiday House, it was about selling my idea to others. Actually, it was more like begging designers and companies to be on board (not an easy task). I never imagined, ten years ago, that this idea would bring the most generous, talented, and knowledgeable people into my world. I want to give a special thanks to those who have stood by my side, unwavering, from Day One, and helped turn my dream into reality.

Holiday House Designers, New York City

Iris Dankner, Jay Dankner

Bradley Theodore, Iris Dankner

Iris Dankner, Martha Stewart

Iris Dankner, Hoda Kotb

Sasha Bikoff, Christopher Hyland, Iris Dankner

Iris Dankner, Katharina Plath

I conceived the idea of Holiday House while I was a member of the board of The Susan G. Komen Race for the Cure. While most of the board members were hesitant to start a new project that cost so much to finance, Blythe Masters, the chairman of the board, was all in. She went above and beyond by putting in the seed money to produce the first Holiday House in 2008. She was the force that got the ball in motion. Blythe, I will never forget your charitable spirit and support.

Miki Schulman, from Manhattan Shade and Glass, helped me by sharing her success stories and tips about how she began fund-raising, and eventually helped me launch Holiday House. Also, Mitchel Schulman showed his support by listening to me and giving me the nudge I needed to get started. That "nudge" I will never forget.

Christina Juarez, you are such a rock star and a publicist extraordinaire. Your connections and expert knowledge were invaluable to me! Thank you for believing in me and always supporting Holiday House.

Stephen Fanuka, contractor with a huge heart, always made sure we were well protected. You are so kind, generous—and handsome. What amazing qualities to find in a contractor!

Maurice Dubois, thank you for always being by my side and teaching me to speak from the heart.

Jennifer Skoda, your guidance and professional business advice have been essential to the growth of Holiday House. Thank you for always being in my corner and being the brains behind the entire operation.

Barbara Schorr, there are no words to express how thankful I am for your love and support. You have been my rock through some of the toughest and most memorable Holiday House catastrophes. We always came out winning, with a smile and a good story. Thank you for always having my back.

Christopher Hyland, my generous, kind, and creative co-chair, thank you for helping me take Holiday House to a new level. It's because of your connections and gracious heart that we were able to come this far. You introduced us to the best designers in the industry, and made the Holiday House journal a work of art. And thank you so much for writing the Foreword to this book. I couldn't think of anyone more meaningful for the job. I love you, Constantino, and everyone at *Hyland Magazine*.

Katharina Plath, you are so much more than a publicist: You are the ultimate connector. Your incredible energy and spirit always make it fun to work together. You are like the mayor of every city we've visited. Everyone knows and loves you. Thank you for always being the force behind the ever-growing success of Holiday House!

Christina Juarez, Stephen Fanuka

Iris Dankner, Venus Williams

Maurice DuBois, Iris Dankner

Jennifer Skoda, Iris Dankner

Iris Dankner, Barbara Schorr

# “EVERY DAY IS A HOLIDAY AF

Iris Dankner, Rio Hamilton

Iris Dankner, Cindy Citrone, Heidi Taylor, Barbara Schorr

Michael Cox, Iris Dankner, Marcus Harris, Steve Smith (NY Giants)

NFL Cancer Survivors photoshoot

Thank you to our P.R. gurus, Jan MacLatchie of JanMacBrands, and Tyler Hamilton and Stephanie Miller of Spread P.R. You brought so much strategic and creative thinking to the house!

Thanks to Rio Hamilton for the many blog posts, social media content, and for being such a good friend.

Emily and Leonard Blavatnik, who made Holiday House possible. I am forever grateful for your benevolence and philanthropy. Thank you for allowing us to grow Holiday House in the Academy Mansion. Special thanks to David Appelson and Laurel Greenman for working with us at the mansion and making all this possible. Jon Siegel and Peter Hornstein, thank you for your patience and helping with installations. You guys are amazing.

To The Breast Cancer Research Foundation®, thank you for your tireless work and for being a vital factor in merging my two passions. I firmly believe that because of the work you do, we will one day live in a world without breast cancer. To Myra Biblowit, thank you for your never-ending efforts to find a cure.

Cindy Citrone—From the day we met we had an intense connection through our love of the Steelers, Carnegie Mellon, and most important, Meredith. The photoshoot of our “team” was a day I will never forget, especially since some of our most special team members are no longer with us. Because of you, the Ultimate Football Room was created and took Holiday House to a new level.

Thank you Alan Barry, Carl Bellavia, Phillip Ennis, and Anastassios Mentis, our room photographers, and Rio Hamilton, Richard Lewin, Patrick McMullen, and Annie Watt, who so wonderfully captured the special energy of our parties and guests.

Patrick J. Hamilton, I am so thrilled that we were able to work together on this book. Your creativity and huge heart make you an incredible person. Always love having you on Team Holiday House!

Jared Seligman, thank you for taking me downtown and keeping me hip! Your spirit and creativity is beyond…It’s our secret that your dream is to be a designer.

Arthur Becker, one of the kindest and smartest men I’ve ever met, thank you for trusting us with your townhouses in SoHo. Working with you has been an unforgettable experience.

And thank you to all the inspired designers, sponsors, and design chairs. It is because of your creativity and generosity that Holiday House has grown to be one of the premiere showhouses in the country.

Iris Dankner, Christopher Hyland

Holiday House Designers, Sag Harbor

Iris Dankner, Iris Apfel, Jared Seligman

# TER YOU SURVIVE CANCER.”

Iris Dankner, Tori Mellott

Holiday House Designers, Hamptons 2014 Kick-off Party

Iris Dankner, Joyce Misrahi, Rachel Laxer

Iris Dankner, Sara Gore

Iris Dankner, Lana Lawrence

There are a few companies that I must single out and thank. From day one they trusted me and helped Holiday House flourish. Roche Bobois, Baccarat, Fendi Casa, Farrow & Ball, Robert Allen, Kravet, Stark, and Lladro. Thank you for always surrounding us with your luxury brands and making us look our best! Special thanks to Robert Allen for sponsoring two amazing rooms that we featured in this book.

I've also met some of my best friends and supporters through Holiday House. Serniqua Dougherty, Charles Pavarini, Daniel Lombardi, and Ally Coulter—you showed me what real support and friendship look like! Special thanks to Ally for taking me on such fun European adventures, sharing lots of laughs and always supporting Holiday House.

*Traditional Home Magazine*, thank you for being our proud media sponsor in New York for so many years. I've loved working with you and your team!

Hamptons Cottages & Gardens, our media sponsor on Long Island, thank you for taking us out East! Special thanks to Marianne Howatson, Pamela Eldridge, and Kendell Cronstrom for all the hard work you have done for Holiday House Hamptons.

Thank you to my team, Stephanie Cain and Shaina Kalin, for always keeping me calm and taking care of so many loose ends. I couldn't do all I do without you. And kudos to Shaina for making this book happen.

Rachel Laxer, Joyce Misrahi, and Grant Pierrus—thank you for turning my dream of taking Holiday House across the pond into a reality. I have truly loved learning from each of you.

Finally, a huge thank you to Pointed Leaf Press. Publishing a book has always been high on my bucket list, but never did I imagine it would be so much fun. Suzy, you and your royal staff, Prince Frederico and Princess Kelly, made this process an incredible experience. Your professionalism and imaginativeness were beyond compare!

Thank you all from the bottom of my heart.

I want to dedicate this book to two dear friends I have met through Holiday House and lost to cancer: Lana Lawrence and Champagne Joy. Lana, I miss our margaritas and laughs. Your warm heart, sense of style, and sense of humor are missed every day! Champagne, your face will be deeply missed at every Holiday House event. You are a true inspiration to so many and you will never be forgotten.

**—IRIS DANKNER, JULY 2017**

Holiday House Designers, Bridgehampton

Amy Lau, Michael Tavano, Ally Coulter

Marianne Howatson, Kendell Cronstrom, Iris Dankner

Joan Rivers, Iris Dankner

Champagne Joy, Iris Dankner

# CREDITS

**PAGE 2 — DÉCOR BY GUILLAUME GENTET, INC.**

2013: The designer transformed the center courtyard of the Academy Mansion into a chic *Women's Day Lounge*—the perfect backdrop for his own wedding to David Carpenter.

**PAGE 4 — BITTT GROUP**

2011: *The Birthday Celebration* dressing room honored the joy, grace, and resiliency of cancer survivors.

**PAGE 6 — PATRICK JAMES HAMILTON DESIGNS**

2014: The designer channeled a Dublin row house with his *Modern St. Patrick's Day* gentlemen's sitting room, with emerald walls and Irish Waterford crystal.

**PAGES 8 AND 13 — ID CREATIONS**

2014: Shell chairs, coral, and a beachy landscape painting brought the Hamptons vibe indoors, in the Holiday House founder's *Bungalow* room.
2014: Dankner created an elegant dressing room for the bride-to-be, to mark her daughter's upcoming wedding.

**PAGE 241 — BARBARA OSTROM & ASSOCIATES**

2010: Before Holiday House was a showhouse, it was a tabletop event, and the designer's exotic dining environment marked the *Chinese New Year.*

**PAGE 247 — UNLIMITED EARTH CARE, INC.**

2016: Vibrant color and sculptural shape with exuberant plantings set against the shingle siding of the exterior, hearkening the *Spring Equinox*.

**OPPOSITE — RIO HAMILTON**

2016: The *bon vivant* set the stage for fun, with a riot of pattern and an oversized Toulouse Lautrec-inspired scene, in his festive *Gentlemen's Lounge.*

**Iris Dankner,** interior designer and breast cancer survivor, is the founder of Mission In Pink, Inc., a non-profit devoted to raising funds to support the fight against breast cancer. In 2008, she founded Holiday House, melding her love for interior design with her passion for helping people fight that dreaded disease. Dankner serves as a Member on the Advisory Board of The Breast Cancer Research Foundation® and served for six years as an Executive Committee Member of the Susan G. Komen Greater NYC Board of Directors.

**Patrick J. Hamilton,** is an interior designer, tastemaker, writer, humorist, and activist living and working in Manhattan. He has appeared on HouseBeautiful.com, HGTV, ApartmentTherapy.com, and in *Traditional Home*. Hamilton spearheaded "It Gets Better: NYC Designing Men," and writes for advertising agencies, design and LGBTQ websites, and for his own blog, AskPatrick.blogspot.com. He made his showhouse debut at Holiday House in 2013.

**Christopher Hyland,** founder of the textile company that bears his name and the digital magazine *HYLAND,* was chairman of the first Presidential Transition Conference on Design. He holds honorary doctorates from the New York School of Interior Design, Kiev Economic University, and the Savannah College of Art & Design. He is chairman of the Advisory Board of the Metropolitan Orchestra Musicians and has been co-chairman and chairman of Holiday House.

PHOTOGRAPHY CREDITS: Miguel Alonso: 253; Jessica Antola: 140–141; Alan Barry: 13, 32–33, 52–55, 136, 148–149, 156–157, 204–219, 226–229; Photos by Carl Bellavia: Opposite half-title–1, 14, 16–17, 24–25, 36–37, 46–47, 56–57, 72–73, 86–87, 98–99, 106–107, 126–127; Carter Berg: 34–35; Brett Beyer: 104–105, 122–123; Michael Croteau: 94–95; Paul Domzal: 130–131, 184–185; Courtesy Douglas Elliman Real Estate: 138–139; Phillip Ennis: 28–29, 44–45, 48–51, 90–91, 108–111, 164–165, 241; Chris Foster: 190–191; John Gruen: 62–65, 120–121; Jonas Gustavsson: 4; Mick Hales: 180–181; Austin Handler: 144–147, 176–179 ; Nick Johnson: 60–61, 70–71, 74–77, 84–85, 116–117, 168–173, 192–193 ; Paul Johnson: 100–101; Jody Kivort: 6, 114–115; Lorin Klaris: 42–43; Hulya Kolabas: 124–125; Peter Kubilus: 80–81; Rick Lew: 88–89, 118–119; Adam Kane Macchia: 188–189; Ric Marder Imagery: 150–151; Peter Margonelli: 102–103; Joshua McHugh: 38–41; Anastassios Mentis: 142–143, 160–163, 166–167, 196–197, 247; Mirra Studios & Read McKendree: 202–203; John Muggenborg: 152–153; Gonzalo Novaro: 198; Marco Ricca©: 2, 18–23, 26–27, 30–31, 92–93, 112–113, 128–129, 132–133, 154–155, 158–159, 174–175; Michael Rodenbush: 82–83; Mark Roskams: 186–187; Alan Schindler: 66–67; Jacob Snavely: 220–223; Rikki Snyder: 8, 182–183, 194–195; Eric Striffler: 68–69; Milton White: 200–201; Vicente Wolf: 96–97, 134–135; Roy Wright: 58–59, 78–79

**POINTED LEAF PRESS, LLC.**

PUBLISHER/EDITORIAL DIRECTOR
**SUZANNE SLESIN**

CREATIVE DIRECTOR
**FREDERICO FARINA**

MANAGING EDITOR
**KELLY KOESTER**

DESIGNER
**DOMINICK SANTISE**

HOLIDAY HOUSE TEN YEARS OF DECORATING FOR A CURE

Pointed Leaf Press, LLC.
136 Baxter Street, New York, NY 10013
www.pointedleafpress.com


Printed and bound in Italy.
First edition
10 9 8 7 6 5 4 3 2 1
Library of Congress Control Number: 2017947925
ISBN: 978-1-938461-46-0

ATES, INC. **WEITZMAN HALPERN INTERIOR DESIGN**
**LLC** ALLY COULTER DESIGNS **AMY LAU DESIGN** A
**EY DARRYL** BALTIMORE DESIGN GROUP **BARBARA**
ROUP **BJÖRN BJÖRNSSON INTERIOR DESIGN, LLC.** BJ
**BIN** BRETT DESIGN, INC. **CAMPION PLATT INTERIO**
**UP** CHARLES J. NAFIE ARCHITECTS **CHARLOTTE**
& KRAVIS, INC. **DARRIN VARDEN DESIGN** DÉCOR
INC. **DONNA LIVINGSTON DESIGN** DREW MCGUKI
**ORS** ELIZABETH BOLOGNINO INTERIORS, LLC.
RNIE, INC. **HARRY HEISSMANN, INC.** HB HOME
**IO** HUNTLEY & CO. INTERIOR DESIGN **ID CREAT**
**OD, LLC.** JAIME WALTERS **JAMES RIXNER, INC.** J
EK & CO. **JOYCE D. SILVERMAN INTERIORS** JUSTI
**ST** MABLEY HANDLER INTERIOR DESIGN **MAD**
TERIORS **MATTHEW PATRICK SMYTH, INC.** MELAN
**GN** PAMELA BANKER ASSOCIATES **PARIS FORINO**
ILTON DESIGNS **PATRICK MCGRATH DESIGN** PAT
**A, LLC.** PAVARINI DESIGN **PLUMRIDGEHOUSE I SU**
NTERIORS **RC STUDIO** RICHARD MISHAAN DES
**MILTON** ROBERT PASSAL INTERIOR & ARCHITE
**ORBAN** SASHA BIKOFF INTERIOR DESIGN **TAM**
NC. **TIMOTHY BROWN STUDIO** TINA RAMCHANDA
**SIGN** 2 MICHAELS DESIGN **UNLIMITED EARTH CA**
ATES, INC. **WEITZMAN HALPERN INTERIOR DESIGN**
**LLC** ALLY COULTER DESIGNS **AMY LAU DESIGN** A